KENYA

KENYA

· THE MAGIC LAND ·

Mohamed Amin · Duncan Willetts · Brian Tetley

THE BODLEY HEAD
LONDON

Acknowledgements
We would like to thank all the many people of Kenya for their kindness, courtesy and willingness to help us in the photography and research for this book; especially Captain Tad Watts of Boskovic Air Charters who flew many missions for us to photograph this beautiful country from the air.

First published 1988 by
The Bodley Head Ltd.,
32 Bedford Square,
London WC1B 3EL

© Camerapix 1988

British Library Cataloguing in Publication Data:
Amin, Mohamed
KENYA, The Magic Land
  1. Kenya — Illustrations
  I. Title   II. Willetts, Duncan
  III. Tetley, Brian
  967.6′204′0222

ISBN 0 370 31225 2

This book was designed and produced by
Camerapix Publishers International,
P.O. Box 45048,
Nairobi, Kenya

Design: Craig Dodd

Printed in Hong Kong by Mandarin Offset.

End papers: Sculpture depicting Kenya's battle for freedom; Half-title: Elephant cropping savannah grassland. On average, the African elephant eats around 140 kilos of fodder a day. Title pages: Maasai, guarding cattle in Amboseli, believe that Enkai, God, gave all the cattle in the world to them. Contents pages: Somali youngster leads camels across Kenya's searing northern deserts.

Contents

1 **Introduction: The Magic Land** 7

2 **Wandering Through Eden** 25
The Kenya Coast

3 **Snows of Kilimanjaro** 55
Tsavo, Amboseli and Maasai Mara

4 **Shantytown Capital** 95
Nairobi and the Rift Valley

5 **Heartland of Kenya** 125
The Aberdares and Mount Kenya

6 **Land of Milk and Honey** 151
Western Kenya and Lake Victoria

7 **Cradle of Mankind** 171
Northern Kenya and Lake Turkana

1·Introduction: The Magic Land

It's a land where the sun should shine all the year round. Astride the Equator, refreshed by the zephyr breezes blown off the Indian Ocean, Kenya is the original tropical paradise.

But sometimes it rains for days on end. And on the highland plateaux, when the black-grey clouds scowl as they come scudding through the giant heather leaving you drenched and cold, it's easy to imagine you are walking on Europe's winter moorlands.

Yet in a second you can walk out of the clouds rolling across the mountain moorlands between 12,000 and 14,000 feet and step under a rainbow. It starts almost where you stand and ends far away, dazzling in its intensity, on the plains below where the rains rarely fall and the desert rolls out of sight beyond an horizon that lies more than 160 kilometres away.

There's no proverbial pot of gold at the end of Kenya's many rainbows — but wherever it falls and wherever you go there is a golden land: rich in the wealth of its contrasts, its landscapes, its cultures and the welcome it extends to all its guests and visitors.

It affects many people in many ways.

You can stand in the relentless glare of the sun in far-distant Suguta Valley, one of the hottest places on earth, and hear only silence; a silence beautiful in the poetry of its lyrics — the whirr of an insect's wings, the sigh of an abandoned breeze, the soft footfall of an unseen animal and the scurry of a scorpion as it disappears beneath a rock.

You can walk a deserted glittering white beach, the breakers combing over the coral reef far offshore, the breeze whispering through waving palms and clusters of bougainvillea and hibiscus as the cloying fragrance of frangipani fills the air.

Camp in the rolling savannah, far from any other human being or settlement, and watch great herds of elephant browsing through the tall lush grasses.

Climb sheer rock faces or study the glory of a million flamingos as they colour the waters of a soda lake shimmering pink.

Go fishing for black bass on the crystal clear waters of a jewelled lake set 6,000 feet above sea level or hang glide from the 11,000-foot brow of the Elgeyo Escarpment with the world in miniature laid out 7,000 feet beneath you.

Tackle an ice cliff at 16,000 feet on Mount Kenya or ride a camel through the unrelenting heat of the scrub thorn of northern Kenya.

Whatever you do, wherever you go, you're almost certain to come to love Kenya's many different faces. And 'Kenya Loves U2' proclaim the car stickers that festoon the country's *matatus*.

These freelance public transport vehicles, some small simple pick-ups which ply the city streets, some large, long-distance coaches which ply the national freeways, carry the farmers, traders and entrepreneurs of this sunny land about their seemingly unceasing travels and business.

It's a display of free-wheeling enterprise and mercantile initiatives, allied to long hours of industriousness and labour, which leaves the observer exhausted simply in watching.

All this, and more, make up the glories of Kenya, a country — for those who know and love it — without peer anywhere in the world.

Kenya in 1988 was not the Kenya of a hundred years ago in which H.

Preceding pages: Less than a century old, Kenya's 'City in the Sun' is the capital Nairobi.

Above: Marble gravestone of veterinarian Captain A. J. Haslam, near Fort Smith on the outskirts of Nairobi; ambushed and killed by a Kikuyu war party on a visit to the Thika area.

Above right: The fig tree, mgumo, *at Fort Smith, near Kabete, Nairobi, planted in 1890 by Britain's first proconsul in East Africa, Frederick Lugard and Chief Kinyanjui, to mark the signing of a peace treaty between the Kikuyu and Britain.*

Rider Haggard's immortal hero Alan Quatermain set out to discover the secrets of *King Solomon's Mines.* Quatermain's adventures enthralled a Victorian world that knew as little of Africa as it did of the far side of the moon. Haggard's century-old imaginings of life and events was as far from the reality of Kenya then as it is today.

And yet . . . under the stars on the hills above Elmenteita, the soda lake in the Rift Valley, where the trail to the fabled mines — an old slave caravan trail from the great lake in the west — still winds through wilderness land, Quatermain's fictional Africa feels close. All it needs is a lively and adventurous imagination and the shadows and sounds of the night take on perspectives close to his.

It's just under a century ago that a small contingent of British officials and soldiers carved a dirt road from the coast through the 500 kilometres of wilderness that lay between Mombasa Island and the flat, dank, foul-smelling swamp called Nyrobi by the Maasai, meaning place of the cold waters.

Beyond that lay the rising shoulders of the eastern wall of the Great Rift Valley cloaked with impenetrable forest. Imperialists and colonizers they may have been, but brave also. A small band cut through the forest for a few kilometres to a place called Kabete which today is the northernmost periphery of the Kenya capital Nairobi, a metropolis that belongs exclusively to the twentieth century.

Here in 1890 they built a fortress — naming it Fort Smith after the first commanding officer — and carved a moat around it and built a stout stockade laced with thorn barbs.

They lived under siege from the crafty, stealthy Kikuyu, rich in forest lore and well versed in military strategy. Walk today a few hundred metres from Fort Smith, now aged and mellow, and you'll come across the marble headstones, untended and neglected in a fallow maize field,

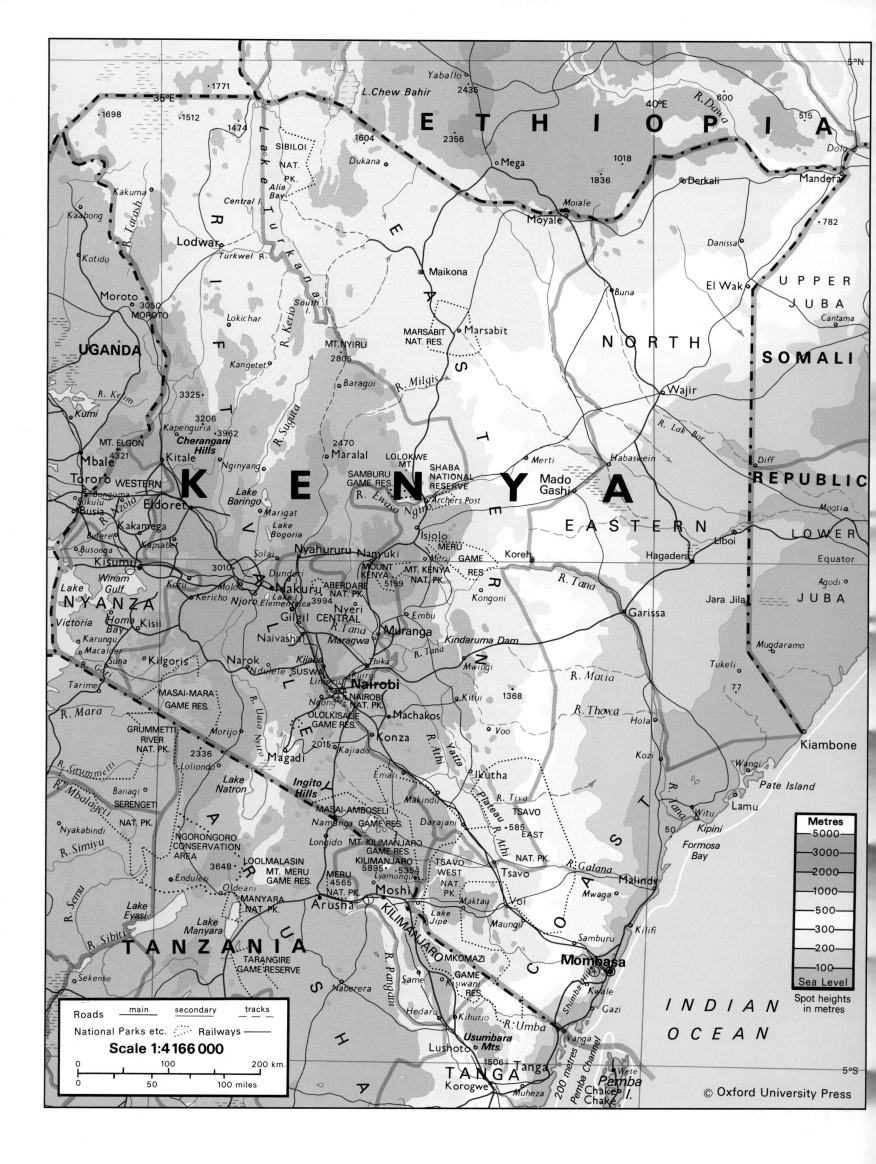

Above: Built between 1896 and 1901, the 1,000-kilometre-long Uganda Railway, from Mombasa on the Indian Ocean to the shores of Lake Victoria, was christened the Lunatic Line.

of three of them — one the victim of the Kikuyu, another of a lioness, the third of a lion.

In 1987, the fig tree, *mugumo*, which the English and the Kikuyu planted near the turn of the century as a symbol of peace between the two peoples, towers forty metres above the compound; and the villagers around Fort Smith, sons and daughters of those Kikuyu warriors, salute the European with a smile and a word of welcome. With independence in 1963, bitterness was laid aside in the joy of nationhood.

To western eyes, Kenya, unstructured and unhomogenized, promising only bountiful harvests, was there for the taking. But the tribal territories in fact were as well defined in the minds of the rulers of these fiefdoms as the shires of England and peopled by stock as proud of their heritage and as independent.

As far as our knowledge of mankind's beginnings extends today, it was in Kenya that mankind's ancestors first stood upright and took those first faltering footsteps to an always uncertain destiny.

The first outsiders venturing into Kenya, ancestors of today's indigenous populations, were nomads and warriors, craftsmen and farmers — moving south from northern Africa down that mighty concourse of history, the Nile, long before the baby Moses rode its waters in a reed basket.

Later came the Arabs and the Europeans and still later new waves of these migrants with the fires of their new-found faiths in their blood.

But until the last 150 years few of these ventured into the interior.

On the map of Kenya — 580,000 square kilometres bisected by the

11

Equator on the eastern seaboard of Africa — the dominant feature, immediately visible, is the great scar of the Rift Valley.

Another is the great lake which marks its western border, Victoria, second largest of the world's freshwater lakes: an inland sea covering 68,800 square kilometres and shared by Uganda and Tanzania as well.

This fabled source of the Nile, whose waters sustained the greatest of man's earliest civilizations, Egypt, more than 5,000 years ago, remained unknown to the outside world until the middle of the last century.

The Rift Valley — a cataclysmic 5,500-kilometre-long gorge in the earth's surface extending from Jordan in the north to Beira in Mozambique in the south — was identified even later. Both were formidable barriers hiding the glories within from the prying eyes of would-be intruders.

For most of 2,000 years the only area of Kenya familiar to the rest of the world was the coast: a long ribbon of land between sixteen and twenty kilometres wide that rises up steeply a thousand feet or more to the first of the great inland escarpments. Like a series of steps, these climb up to the great highland massif of central Kenya before descending in another series of steps to Lake Victoria.

Warm and humid, tempered by the gentle monsoons sweeping up from the south or from the Arabian and Indian coasts in the north, it was a place for indolence. Fish could be plucked from the sea. Fruit grew in profusion. The lotus eater found paradise.

The first record of the Kenya coast is contained in a second-century geography produced by the Egyptian scientist Ptolemy, drawn vividly from the legends and anecdotes of ancient mariners whose voyages had taken them along the coast.

Mombasa was the prize of the East African coast, a haven to the dhow captains who traded between the Gulf and Azania, *Land of the Blacks*, long

Above: Oil painting depicting Jomo Kenyatta's arrest at his Gatundu home in Kiambu district at midnight on 20 October 1952 — the start of a seven-year-long incarceration in Kenya's northern wilderness. Mzee Kenyatta endured his long ordeal to lead his country to independence in 1963. Widely acclaimed as Africa's greatest statesman, he was universally mourned when he died on 22 August 1978.

Above: Multi-racial Kenya is made up of more than forty different ethnic communities. A lively youngster from the minority Asian community joins the Independence Day festivities.

before the birth of Christ: sailing on the northerly monsoons in their handsome and sturdy high-prowed vessels with cargoes of porcelain, silks and spices, returning on the southerly monsoon with ambergris, ivory, gold, gems and slaves. North of Mombasa's natural harbour were Malindi and the Lamu archipelago, other mercantile princedoms where the dhow masters traded.

The Coast's golden age began with the arrival of Islam around the ninth century and gave rise to a glorious cultural and architectural heritage. The cultural heritage still lives, colourful and strong. The architectural glory remains in the weathered ruins of royal cities buried in tangles of tropical undergrowth.

But of all the migrants, settlers and visitors who stepped ashore in the thousand years between AD 900 and 1900, only a handful ventured into the unknown hinterland: some to die of disease, others bound up in tribal disputes, others as intruders on sacrosanct territory.

For the British a mixture of empirical pride, exploration and Christian conscience was triple inspiration for venturing forth into the 'Dark Continent'.

Missionary causes — evangelism and the abolition of slavery — were the most celebrated and they inspired others, like the young Scotsman Joseph Thomson who undertook an epic journey through Kenya in 1883: one which extended over fifteen months and took him virtually the length and breadth of what is today Kenya.

He came as a peaceful mercenary, commissioned by the Royal Geographical Society of Britain to establish the truth — or otherwise — of missionary reports that snow existed on the Equator.

Assembling an expedition of fewer than 150 porters and commissaries in Zanzibar — in the face of Stanley's advice to 'take a thousand men or die' in the warrior kingdoms of the Maasai — Thomson, then twenty-six, landed on a beach on the south coast in March 1883 and set forth on an odyssey as remarkable for its humour as its adventure. He collected a treasury of anecdotes and information which still fuel the imagination today.

If anything, he was Kenya's first tourist — marching through the inhospitable wastes of the Taru Desert and on to the Tsavo and Amboseli game plains beneath the lofty, snow-white splendour of Kilimanjaro, Africa's highest mountain.

He maintained an uneasy peace with the Maasai who were fascinated by his white skin and the many unusual trinkets that he carried: water that boiled in an instant, an effect created with Enos fruit salts, and his false teeth.

Keeping a steady distance between himself and the following Maasai, Thomson marched on from the base of Kilimanjaro to Lake Naivasha, in the shadows of the extinct volcano Longonot, and then up the eastern wall of the Rift Valley to the 12,000-foot heights of the Nyandarua mountain massif.

It was there, as he crested the moorlands early one morning, that Mount Kenya — Kirinyaga, sacred peak of the Kikuyu, the abode of God, *Ngai* — shed its veils of mist and revealed the startling glory of its eternal necklace of ice: glistening glaciers astride the Equator beneath the twin peaks of Batian and Nelion which, at 17,058 feet, is second in Africa only 13

Left: Schoolchildren gather around Kenya's national flag — black for the people of Kenya, green for the fertile land, and red for the blood of those who died to win Kenya's freedom.

Below: Young Boni woman, member of a nomadic community of hunter-gatherers, with water gourd.

to Kilimanjaro.

From there he ventured northward along the floor of the Rift to Lake Baringo and then up the precipitous western wall of the Rift, the awesome Elgeyo escarpment, to the moorlands of Mount Elgon, reaching up to 14,170 feet, returning through the western plains of Kenya on the shores of Lake Victoria to the coast. By any standards, it was a monumental feat of endurance and enterprise. It heralded the birth of modern Kenya.

He had covered a vast area and met people of many different cultures. More than forty different ethnic groups make up the mosaic of modern Kenya, all united under the national green, black, and red flag — green for the land, black for the people and red for the blood shed in the fight for freedom — and the national motto, *Harambee*, meaning 'Let's All Pull Together'.

15

Opposite: Thorn stockade and thatched mud rondavels atop a domed hill exemplify a traditional Kenya farm compound.

Above: Golden palm weaver spins a basket-like nest from fronds and grass.

Above right: Known as the 'chamois of Africa', a tiny klipspringer. Weighing no more than eighteen kilos, the antelope is able to walk up steep rock faces and is a phenomenal jumper — its thick coat cushioning the shock of hitting rock walls.

Though a century ago there was no conscious national ethos, seventy-five years of divide-and-rule by the British had the very effect the policy was meant to suppress. The people came together as one.

It created a nation of harmonious contrasts: all the major African ethnic groups are represented in the nation's citizens, as are the Arab, Asian and European migrants who came and settled.

The landscapes, flora and fauna are as diverse — and as magnificent — as the people. One-third of Kenya is arid or semi-arid desert: barren, brown, burnt-out land which is hauntingly beautiful.

One-third is highland, mountain and forest, lake and farmland, much of it fertile and bountiful.

The remaining third is savannah grassland — home of the last remaining great wildlife spectacle in the world, where creatures which evolved more than 100 million years ago still flourish; creatures such as the crocodile and the rhinoceros, threatened only by predatory, avaricious man and, conversely, protected by the same species, albeit all too often inadequately.

Kenya first became the protectorate of British East Africa in July 1895 after the Imperial British East Africa Company, founded by Sir William Mackinnon, became insolvent. It remained a protectorate until 1920, when it was established as a Crown Colony — a status that lasted only forty-three years.

A thrifty Scotsman, Sir William sought both to fight the slave trade and at the same time turn a penny or two out of the enterprise. He wanted to build a mercantile company equal to that of the British East India Company. But in a land where there were no communications his projects never matched the grandeur of his ambition.

The key to penetrating the interior, of course, was a railway to the great lake, Victoria — a thousand kilometres away across, and over,

17

Opposite: Considered by many the most beautiful of Kenya's wild cats, the leopard's sandy coat is covered with dark rosettes — not spots. Although hunted ruthlessly for their coats, their elusive and solitary habits have helped them survive even in well-settled farm and suburban areas.

Above: Tawny and eager, two young lion cubs begin to explore the wilderness.

some of the most hostile terrain in the world.

Sir William launched the Central Africa Railway to achieve this ambition — with a track and rolling stock best described as the 'Toy Town Railway'.

It was the British Government which took up the challenge seriously in 1895, commissioning the Uganda Railway, an incredible feat of construction dubbed 'The Lunatic Line' by Parliamentary critics in Whitehall.

Few enterprises in the history of civil engineering can match the drama, courage and initiative of this achievement — completed over six years at a cost of many human lives and £5 million, an immense sum for those times.

It was the key which opened the door to Kenya, drawing a wave of immigrants and creating the cosmopolitan ambience which still distinguishes Nairobi where the railway arrived on 30 May 1899 — 500 kilometres from Mombasa and three years after the first rail had been laid.

All that distinguished the Nairobi railhead, apart from the swamp, were the stables run by a Royal Engineers sergeant, George Ellis.

Below: One of the regular Sunday races at Nairobi's forest-lined Ngong racecourse.

Sidings, marshalling yards and workshops sprang up and in the van of the railway came the camp followers — prostitutes, carpetbaggers, traders, labourers and business men — from every corner of the world.

Little more than eighty years later, a United Nations headquarters city, capital of much of east and central Africa as well as Kenya, Nairobi's population — officially a million, unofficially more than two million — was projected to reach four million when it was a century old.

Thirty months after reaching Nairobi — on 20 December 1901 — Florence Preston, wife of Ronald Preston who led the construction work all the way, hammered home the last key of the track overlooking Lake Victoria. Around this last railhead sprang up Kenya's third largest town, Kisumu, with a population projected at around half a million people a century later.

Three years after the railway's completion Britain's proconsul to Kenya, Sir Charles Eliot, an ascetic, aloof, scholarly man, pronounced that though many railways had opened up a country, the Uganda Railway had literally created a nation.

Throughout, despite pressure from the white settlers and British representatives including Eliot, Britain stood fast to its principle that the interests of the indigenous Kenyans remained paramount.

Yet Independence was achieved only after one of the dourest and longest freedom fights in African history.

Colonialism introduced modern education and technology, swiftly accepted and adapted by Kenyans. After freedom in 1963, these were blended into Kenya's own ageless structures of justice, democracy and administration.

The seed for national government was sown on 17 August 1907, the day when the first meeting of Kenya's Legislative Council — sadly without an African member — was held in the tin-and-timber Railway Institute in Nairobi where the Railway Club now stands, on Ngong Road, just off Uhuru Highway.

One of the first Acts passed that day was the abolition of slavery at the Kenya Coast — and the introduction of hanging as the official means of capital punishment.

Kenya's first independent national Parliament arose out of the Legislative Council and became active after the national flag was raised at midnight in the first minute of 12 December 1963.

Even then, the only permanent way to Nairobi and Kisumu remained the railway. Just a few hundred kilometres of metalled road existed at the birth of Independent Kenya. For the rest travel was either by air or dirt and gravel roads. Many remote areas had no link with the rest of country.

Change was swift and stunning. Twenty years after Independence, Kenya had more than 20,000 kilometres of modern highways. Electric power had penetrated deep into the rural areas. New hospitals had arisen. Public health services were free and so was primary education — even with a population growing at the rate of around four per cent a year, the highest birth rate in the world.

Just as dramatic was the progress in wildlife and nature conservation. On the foundation of the twelve national parks and game reserves the new nation inherited from its colonial overlords, Kenya was to build one 21

of the most impressive conservation programmes in the world.

In 1988 the country boasted more than sixty nature sanctuaries — national parks and reserves — and protected forest areas. At least ten per cent of the country's natural land resources were dedicated to conservation with laws prohibiting hunting, timber felling and exploitation.

Yet, despite the spread of people and the development of smallholdings, much of Kenya remains as pristine and beautiful as when Joseph Thomson first strode through it. The visitors who have followed in his wake number countless millions.

Five nations share their borders with Kenya: Somalia, Ethiopia and Sudan in the north, Uganda in the west, and Tanzania in the south.

The country's wildlife boasts more than eighty major species including the Big Five — lion, leopard, elephant, buffalo and rhino — and the richest avifauna in Africa, the third richest in the world.

It boasts twenty mountain peaks that rise above 6,500 feet and five great massifs rising above 10,000 feet including majestic 17,058-foot-high Mount Kenya which was once at least 10,000 feet taller before weather eroded it; Mount Elgon at 14,178 feet and the Nyandarua (Aberdares) at 13,120 feet.

Lakes stud the country's Rift Valley — from 6,400-square-kilometre Lake Turkana, the Jade Sea, through Baringo, Bogoria, Nakuru, Naivasha, Elmenteita, to the soda lake Magadi.

Its largest river, the Tana, leaps down the slopes of Mount Kenya and the Aberdares to flow for more than 700 kilometres to the Indian Ocean.

Above: Potential Kenya Olympic gold medallists compete in a national event. Kenya's middle- and long-distance track runners have earned worldwide fame as some of the greatest of all time.

Above: Kenya's five-day, 4,000-kilometre-long Safari Rally, held every Easter, is reckoned the toughest test of man and motorcar as the world's greatest rally drivers tackle sea level terrain and mountain heights of more than 10,000 feet — as well as billowing dust and monsoon downpours.

In the Aberdares, the Gura Falls sways to and fro in the wind as it plummets more than a thousand feet.

These wonders of snow and desert, man and creature, still much as they were milleniums ago, are so stunningly beautiful and varied — the world in microcosm — that they draw the breath of most.

During the 1980s more than half a million tourists a year visited the land where mankind took his first faltering footsteps so long ago, on the shores of Lake Turkana in the country's far north, to enjoy now something of the world that existed then — something of this magic land, Kenya.

2·Wandering Through Eden

Left: Modern heart of Mombasa, Kenya's oldest city.

Below: Former Sultan of Zanzibar's mainland home at Likoni on Kenya's south coast.

Above: Massive ramparts of Mombasa's fifteenth-century Fort Jesus.

the town, drawing too little water to have need of the deeper anchorages in Kilindini Creek to the south of the island.

Mombasa was rich in gold and ivory from the beginning and, near the end of the fifteenth century, these marked it out as a prize for the fleets of the Portuguese whose greatest navigator, Vasco da Gama, sailed in the service of King John and his son, Prince Henry 'The Navigator'. In 1497 King John ordered da Gama to round the Cape and find the sea route to India.

A year later the Portuguese fleet entered Mombasa harbour but was repulsed by the Arabs, whose guerilla fleet cut the anchor ropes of the Portuguese ships. Da Gama sailed on to Malindi to a royal welcome from the local sultan: a monument marking the spot where he stepped ashore still stands on a coral cliff at Silversands.

Mombasa suffered for its reprisal. Two years later Cabral sailed behind da Gama and sacked the town. Five years later, in 1505, another Portuguese mariner, Almeida, came to plunder, followed twenty-three years later by the pillaging sailors of Nuna da Cunha. They found the island port a 'very fair place', praising the work of the masons and carpenters and the 'many fine garments of silk and gold' worn by the men and women.

Finally, the Portuguese occupied Mombasa and, during the five years from 1593 to 1598, built the brooding bastion of Fort Jesus overlooking the entrance to the old harbour, where its ramparts and battlements, weathered over 400 years, still remain — silent witness to the town's turbulent history.

Above: Kilifi Creek, nirvana for nature lovers and water sports buffs.

They were stormy centuries for Mombasa and its inhabitants earning it a name as the Island of War. Entrenched within the towering walls and armed with stout cannon and shot, the Portuguese used the fortress as a base from which to spread out and colonize the coastal strip.

Arab resistance was strong. They attacked from sea and land but even when backed by the forces of the Turkish corsair Ali Bey were unable to shake loose the tenacious grip of the Portuguese.

The first of Kenya's European colonizers remained for a century — defying sieges and disease, victualled almost entirely by convoys sailing from Goa in India where they had established another enclave.

But Fort Jesus finally fell to the Arabs in 1699 after its occupants had endured almost three years of siege — beginning on 15 March 1696 when an Arab fleet bombarded the town and 2,500 citizens and fifty Portuguese sought sanctuary within the massive four-metre-thick walls. Relieved by reinforcements from India in September 1697, the beleaguered garrison held out for another fifteen months until the Arabs, aided by the captain and crew of a passing Welsh vessel, scaled the walls. Plague, disease and famine had taken terrible toll. Only thirteen of the people inside the Fort survived — eleven men and two women. The merciless Arabs ran them through immediately. Finally, in 1720 the last Portuguese garrison left the Kenya Coast for good.

Despite their changing dynasties, the Arabs again held dominion and continued to do so until the closing years of the nineteenth century. The islands of Zanzibar and Pemba were part of the Indian Ocean fiefdom of the Sultans of Oman, but control was so weak and ineffective that their power passed into the hands of the squabbling governors they had appointed. The region fell into decline until the 1822 arrival of Sultan Seyyid Said from Oman, who put down the Mazrui dynasty's chiefs and reasserted control of his potentially rich and profitable 'possessions'.

Around this time a British ship, HMS *Leven*, visited Mombasa, and the embattled Mazruis begged Captain Owen to hoist the British flag over Fort Jesus. On 7 February 1824, the British officer proclaimed Mombasa a British 'protectorate' and the Union Jack fluttered over the old battlements. For their part the Mazruis agreed to the abolition of slavery.

Owen, well pleased with his Christian crusade, appointed his first officer, Lieutenant J. J. Reitz, as proconsul — assisted by one interpreter, four sailors and four marines — signalled London and India for ratification of the agreement and set sail.

By such casual negotiation did Britain begin to exercise its influence in East Africa. In the history of empire there can be few instances to match this cursory presumption of imperial power which ultimately, albeit through years of indifference and *laissez faire*, led to Kenya's colonization.

Reitz died of malaria contracted during a mainland visit in May 1824 and was succeeded by a Lieutenant Emery. The British garrison had no armoury or troops to enforce its token rule, and Whitehall sat on Owen's protectorate agreement for three years doing nothing — then repudiated it.

Thus Britain relinquished its first brief foothold in Kenya — not returning to lay its imprint, first on Mombasa and then remorselessly inland, until more than half a century later.

The British presence was established in the person of the Scots

entrepreneur Sir William Mackinnon. In 1887 he was granted an administrative and trading concession under the name of the 'British East Africa Association' and the following year, the Imperial British East Africa Company — IBEA — was incorporated under a Royal Charter.

But the IBEA was bankrupt by July 1895 and was bought out by the British Government for £200,000. Thus began sixty-eight years of Crown rule in Kenya: all but — nominally at least — for the Coast. Until Independence it remained part of the Sultanate of Zanzibar, but in 1888 the Sultan had been 'persuaded' to cede it to the British as a protectorate in return for an annual 'rent' of £17,000.

Today the old Sultan's mainland palace still overlooks the Indian Ocean from its Likoni vantage point across Kilindini Creek; then tranquil and unspoilt but since transformed, by the need to build and supply the Uganda Railway, into what is now the busiest port between Capetown and the Horn of Africa.

Most European visitors once took the leisurely way of Churchill on the three-week-long sea cruise through the Mediterranean, down the Suez Canal and along the Red Sea, to round the Horn of Africa and sail along the Somalia coast to Kenya.

No more: the regular passenger liner services faded out of existence at the end of the 1960s and now only the increasing volume of sea-bound cargoes occupies the Kenya Ports Authority. Today the package tours arrive daily aboard the chartered wide-body jets in a sudden eight-hour transition from winter-bound Europe to South Seas idyll.

In the shadows of Fort Jesus lies the first evidence of Britain's serious intent in Kenya, Mombasa Club. In 1985, within its genteel exterior, the now multi-racial membership celebrated its centennial.

Not far away, in Treasury Square, stand other architectural remembrances of Britain's tenure in Kenya — law courts and banks. On the headland overlooking Fort Jesus is State House, once a resort retreat for the British Governor. Nearer the bustling town centre stands the Anglican Cathedral commemorating Archbishop Hannington, murdered in Uganda on a missionary journey before the turn of the century.

It overlooks the town's oldest hotel, the Manor, little changed in ninety years. Around the corner is another famous hostelry, the Castle, whose pavement cafe is the mandatory social focus of the downtown port and resort retreat: the place to be seen sipping coffee in the morning or sundowners in the early evening.

These early twentieth-century European buildings contrast sharply with the 1980s high-rises beginning to spring up all over the city centre; and also with the elegant Arabian houses of the middle ages in the Old Town, which still retains its Arabian Nights ambience. Studded between them are countless mosques, where the faithful are summoned to prayer by the muezzin, sometimes the high-pitched call of a boy soprano. Hindu temples, one topped by a spire of solid gold and with heavy doors of solid silver, counterpoint the prevailing mixture of Muslim, Hindu and Christian faiths.

This vivid contrast of architecture and ambience melds with the colourful cultures which characterize steamy Mombasa, fusing with the changing cultures and colours of the package tourists who stream in constantly for visits of two to three weeks. A heady and exotic

Above: Pokomo boatman on the Tana River. The 50,000-strong Pokomo community's villages are raised on stilts to avoid the seasonal floods that rage down the Tana.

Left: Low tide on the Kenya Coast, where life is an idyllic existence — its pace adapted to the all-embracing humid heat tempered by the gentle ocean breezes and day-long sunshine.

Below: Sun, sea and sand — part of the Kenya magic.

37

atmosphere, supplemented by the vibrant extrovert population, it gives the town the most exciting night-life — discos and day-and-night clubs — in the country.

South of the island, the visitor discovers a ribbon of lagoons and flawless beaches strung together like pearls upon a string. A new suspension bridge to cross Kilindini Creek to the Likoni mainland — Kenya's own Golden Gate — is on the drawing boards in Tokyo, but for the moment the introduction to this tropical paradise straight from the bookshelves of popular romances is by motor ferry: despised only by those accustomed to the frenzied pace of the western world's major cities.

Handsome Giriama and Digo people, with fine-boned profiles, in casual *kikois* and vivid shirts and blouses, mingle by the waiting line of vehicles amid an uproar of peanut and ice cream vendors and the blaring horns of *matatus* and buses touting for passengers.

In the middle of the creek a cruise liner makes a stately passage upstream to a mooring, as a freighter, heavy-laden with Kenya coffee and tea, steams downstream; outward bound for Europe.

Above: The wide sweep of Malindi bay.

Below: Miracle of the inner universe: lambent yellow profile of a dolphin on the back of a beautifully-coloured yellow-spotted angelfish.

Above: Weaving through translucent surface waters of a Kenya lagoon, a blue angelfish follows in the wake of a soldier fish.

Above: Lionfish displays its dorsal crest in a lagoon.

At Likoni the traffic roars off the ferry avoiding the pedestrian passengers streaming up the concrete slipway in a confusion of pye-dogs, cyclists, kiosks and bus touts.

Kenya's early Europeans made Likoni's modest Shelley Beach their first resort, fanning out slowly southwards. First to Waa, secluded and discreet, where upcountry folk maintain a line of cottages on the cliffs above their own private piece of Eden; then to Tiwi, a mixture of self-service chalets and beach cottages, down-market from the more recent five-star hotels that characterize the next beach, Diani.

It's separated from its northern neighbour by the Mwachema River estuary, focal point of an abandoned scheme to turn Diani into one of the most glittering resorts in the world. Designers and landscape planners devised a scheme to dam the estuary and turn it into a man-made lagoon. But perhaps these beaches are best left as nature shaped them.

Strolling along these silver sands, corrugated by the tide's ebb and flow, looking out at low water across the burnished waters of the lagoon unspoilt by predator or pollution, there's a sense of detachment from the pace and pressures of the real world. The reef that stretches virtually the length of the East African coastline, second only to Australia's Great Barrier Reef, creates a natural sea wall sealing out sharks and oil spills.

From this superlative beach, there's always plenty of depth of water for swimming or goggling. Beneath the placid surface, an inner universe of strange rock formations and marine flora, swaying weeds and sculptured corals dazzlingly lit by the shoals of angel, jewel, lion, zebra, and parrot fish that swarm in and around these underwater gardens, iridescent in their rainbow colours, awaits discovery. This, surely, is the vestibule of paradise.

Behind the beach, scrub jungle, punctuated by coconut and citrus groves, leads inland to patches of remnant tropical forest of which Jadini, dappled and gloomy even in the midday light, is the most extensive. Here, at the soft footfall of an advancing stranger, deadly mambas and cobras vanish into the carpet of fallen leaves and foliage on the jungle floor, colobus monkeys and baboons explode through the trees in a flurry of barking alarm, and a rare, startled antelope leaps fitfully away. Only the myriad butterflies flitting through the motes of light remain undisturbed by the intruders.

Bird life is prolific. Kenya ranks third in the world for the number of species it hosts, most more visible than in the jungles of Latin America, which claim precedence.

Moving so close to nature in its timeless forms imposes a sense of reverence. It's not surprising that some of these forest groves, *keyas*, are regarded as shrines by the local Digo people, who often gather in the shadows of *Kaya Tiwi*, which serves as a cathedral in which to make their supplications to their creator.

Muslims, similarly affected by the spiritual atmospherics, adapted a grove of baobabs, that strange and ubiquitous tree of the tropics, atop a coral cliff as a pilgrims' mosque in the sixteenth century.

Long ago strong tides carved deep caves beneath these cliffs now festooned with thousands of bats that swarm in the swift shutter of nightfall. Throughout the year, day's even tempo close to the Equator barely falters from its almost flawless symmetry of day and night: in

twelve months the daytime extremes vary by only thirty minutes. Nature's creatures function well in this ordered rhythm, confused only when there is an eclipse.

Above: Shy Muslim girls with smiling eyes in the bui-bui, *the traditional Islamic dress.*

The greatest of these primal coastal forests, however, lies a few kilometres inland on the crest of the 1500-foot-high Shimba Hills, long a national reserve known best for its sable antelope. The transition from languid tropical shore to a vestige of upcountry Kenya takes no longer than the brief twenty-minute drive to Kwale, administrative centre of most of the south coast, refreshingly cool after the sweltering heat below. Fanned thousands of kilometres across the Indian Ocean, the monsoon breezes hit the base of the hills and sweep upward to blow across these lush parklands, favoured by the antelope, buffalo and herds of elephant which browse and graze in their protected environment.

Within the forest, thick lianas, grotesque parodies of sculptured forms, festoon themselves around the ancient giants that provide shade and secrecy. Here the lithe leopard stalks unseen, its mottled coat blending perfectly with the shadow and substance of the forest.

In one corner of this sanctuary, linked by walkways above the forest floor, a luxury lodge provides a unique experience. By the light of

40

Above: Member of one of Kenya's least-known communities, the Segeju, a young girl grinds coconut.

artificial moons, enthralled spectators watch the nightly pageant beneath them — elephants coming to water and the smaller creatures, Bambi-like gazelle and antelope, twitching fearfully, alert for the sudden pounce of the most stealthy of all the predators.

Early in the morning, still rapt in the memory of nature's eternal game of kill or be killed, the visitor returns to the contrasts below.

Southwards from Diani, the coast is virtually undeveloped, little affected by the swift growth of Kenya's tourist industry — the second largest revenue earner of the nation's industries — until it reaches Shimoni, the first permanent British settlement on the Kenya mainland. Headquarters of Sir William Mackinnon's enterprise, IBEA and long established as a settler's resort, it's famous as the home of deep-sea big game fishing in the unparalleled reaches of the Pemba channel.

This deep strait, prolific in the catches it yields to the enthusiast, divides the coast from Pemba, the clove island of neighbouring Tanzania. Veterans of the sport from all over the world gather at the Pemba Channel Fishing Club, once favoured with a visit from writer Ernest Hemingway, to test themselves against the giants of the deep — ranging up to 400 kilograms — marlin, barracuda, bonito, tunny, sword, sail and shark.

Just a few kilometres offshore lies one of the world's first marine national parks: gin clear with fascinating coral gardens. There's also an original tropical island, Wasini, inhabited but remote and bedecked by incredible coral formations.

On the mainland there's an old slaving pen where the unfortunates were held, waiting for the slave traders and their ships to arrive there to be locked beneath decks in inhuman conditions, many to die on the long voyage to the western world. It's a part of the Kenya coast that slumbers on, unaffected by the dynamic changes on many stretches of the north coast.

Mass tourism is a relatively recent phenomenon in Kenya. At the time of Independence in the early 1960s, roughly 60,000 visitors a year arrived, some an elite cadre of the wealthy and the famous. Their preference was big game hunting on the inland savannah. Few visited the coast, favoured only by long-term upcountry European farmers and settlers.

For years the northern springboard from Mombasa was a toll bridge floating on pontoons that rose and fell with the tide. Today an elegant new Japanese single-span arch bridges Tudor Creek, dramatic evidence of the transformation that Independence and package tourism have wrought, taking residents and tourists out along a trail that by tarmac, gravel, dirt road, ferry and boat, stretches more than 400 kilometres to the Somalia border.

Half a century ago, a group of investors began to develop the Nyali mainland directly opposite the Old Town. A British administrator from Bombay, Sir Bartle Frere, left his name on one unique settlement at Nyali, Freretown, which he established as a sanctuary for runaway slaves.

Now spacious and gracious houses, an eighteen-hole golf course and smart hotels, of which the oldest and arguably the most splendid is Nyali Beach, grace this stretch of coastline and spin on into the neighbouring beaches, Bamburi and Shanzu.

Just a kilometre or so inland stands a cement factory, once the tenth largest in the world, which wrought hideous disfiguration of the shrub and coral — carving out great quarries. Yet out of that, inspired by a civic conscience that should serve as an exemplar for others, the cement company has initiated one of the most inspiring rehabilitation and conservation schemes in industrial history.

In the late 1960s Swiss agronomist Rene Haller became their landscape and wildlife architect. Two decades later many of the unsightly quarries have been transformed into stunning sanctuaries of casuarina and pine, fish ponds and wildlife retreats — earning revenue as a provider of agricultural and fish produce and as tourist attraction.

Beyond this extensive resort area, a suspension bridge leaps across the mirror surface of Mtwapa Creek. Years ago, however, the road veered inland to a place called Shimo la Tewa, where a hand-hauled rope ferry was manoeuvred by a dusky crew singing ballads in the style of Paul Robeson. Marinas and water sport centres line Mtwapa's deep waters — ideal for scuba diving and water-skiing — rarely ruffled by a breeze, protected by the cliffs on either side, where elegant bungalows stand, their gardens fragrant with the scents of tropical plants.

On the northern side, there's an aquarium and a base for luxury dhow cruises during which the passengers are entertained by Giriama dancers. These exuberant and outgoing people, like the Digo, are members of the ethnic group known collectively as either the Nyika or the Mijikenda. Seven other tribes — Duruma, Jibana, Ribe, Kambe, Rabai, and Kauma, all less well-known — also belong to this million-strong group, but the Giriama are by far the largest.

Somewhere around the sixteenth century, after the Oromo warriors of north-east Kenya and south-east Ethiopia drove them southward, the Giriama moved to the coastal region, setting up a series of fortified hilltop villages.

For centuries the villages, *kaya*, remained distinct from each other, only merging into one corporate community half a century or so ago. They were places where the Giriama seers, a freemasonry of witch doctors, maintained a monopoly on knowledge and medicine, holding the rest in thrall.

Today their thatched houses and easygoing ways, exemplified by their sunny humour and their dances, are vivid reminders of their ancient culture. For centuries, too, their womenfolk understandably went topless in the enervating climate of the coast, the principle point of sexual attraction being considered a well-rounded, not to say enormous, but well-covered posterior. This was frequently enhanced by the addition of padding; the arrival of the bicycle tyre and inner tube early in the century gave great scope for creative beautification in this area of the anatomy.

Many of the Giriama, through centuries of association with the cosmopolitan visitors to the coast, intermarried and became a fusion of mixed origins now identified as the Swahili people. These happy-go-lucky hybrids are devout Muslims and have an aversion to immodest dress, however innocent its intent. Together, however, these different groups give Mombasa and the coast its own distinctive personality, unlike any you will find elsewhere in Kenya.

Above: Giriama children grinding flour. One of the nine tribes which make up the one-million-strong Mijikenda group, Giriama communities are found all along the coast from the Tanzanian border north to Lamu.

One of Kenya's earliest coast resorts was established at Kikambala, just beyond Mtwapa, where the original, airy, high-pitched thatch hotels favoured for their simplicity and coolness have been developed into massive package tour hotels — with blocks of concrete annexes for rooms, service areas, and entertainment — to the regret of most. Still, some developers have stayed true to the concept of tall, timber elegance topped with a thatch of palm fronds, *makuti*.

Lolling on the beach beneath a shady palm just above the high-water mark, vermouth — shaken but not stirred — in hand, watching the tanned, leggy beauties from frozen Europe sway with undulating grace out to the lagoon, while haggling with a passing fisherman over the price of a luscious crayfish, it's easy to fancy you've stepped into the world of James Bond.

After Kikambala, the coast remains unchanged until Kilifi — halfway point between Mombasa and Malindi — except for the sprawling Vipingo sisal estates. One of the earliest cash crops introduced to Kenya, man-made fibres have made sisal production a speculative and often ruinous proposition. It's said, however, that one good year in ten more than compensates the producer. Many have become millionaires overnight when the market booms.

Kilifi, where the antiquated vehicle ferries often create traffic jams kilometres long, is nonetheless one of the jewels of the coast. High cliffs line the entrance to this natural deep-water harbour, only the entrance through the reef limiting the draught of vessels capable of mooring within.

Gracious houses, fit for the Mediterranean Riviera, step down the cliffs overlooking the ocean-going yachts bobbing at their moorings below. Stretching inland some fifteen kilometres, Kilifi serves as a natural water sports arena with wind surfing, water-skiing, powerboat racing and sailing among the prime attractions. It lures other *aficionados* too, including bird buffs. At the far end of the creek the mangrove swamps play host to millions of carmine bee-eaters, which swoop in at dusk in a great cloud, cutting out the light like a darkening storm.

After capturing the bee, these incredible diminutives carefully tap the venomous sting out before swallowing it. With their long beaks, tapering bodies, and elongated tails, in great congregations the sound of their wings fills the air with a vibrant humming noise.

Close by this ornithological treasure house is another, also rich in rare fauna — Sokoke Forest, last of the great indigenous coastal forests. Imperilled though protected, it's still a welcome home for remnant species.

Thatched villages slumber drowsily on between Kilifi and Watamu, the next major resort, their life styles little changed over the years, unaffected by the increasing numbers of tourists. At Takaungu, close to the forgotten grave of an Omani sultan who died here in the nineteenth century, a traditional wood-carving industry thrives, turning out intricately carved doors with Arabic inscriptions.

One of the world's great living languages, Swahili initially was a fusion of Arabic and indigenous vernaculars. Like all great languages it continues to borrow freely from others. Urdu words, like *gari* for vehicle, have an intrinsic place in this fusion — as do English words. For

43

instance, when the British arrived there was no word for Commissioner. Now it has been adapted phonetically as *Komishona*.

The language grew and developed in places like the lost city of Gede, whose ruins lie in the scrub jungle close to Watamu. An elegant capital, it vanished inexplicably in the sixteenth century, swallowed up by the voracious fast-growing trees and lianas, to lie undiscovered until earlier this century.

The ruins show it was inhabited by a cultured and gracious community, but no records survive to reveal its history or why, virtually overnight, it was abandoned. Walking through the relics of these old buildings it's not difficult to sense the brooding spirits that remain. As you pace through the ruins of its old mosques and houses, bats swoop through the dank air and snakes slither silently out of sight under the crumbling walls.

Watamu is set around Turtle Bay, a curve of aquamarine water, coral gardens, and atolls, sweeping inland into the recesses of Mida Creek, another ornithological haven, where bird lovers delight in the richness of resident and migratory species particularly water birds from the northern hemisphere.

Above: Tropical undergrowth overtakes the crumbling ruins of the lost city of Gede, a fabled Arabian town deserted centuries ago.

Scuba divers, for their part, delight in the rich discoveries of Turtle Bay. At high water it's possible to visit an underwater cave where giant rock cod, *tewa*, weighing up to 400 kilograms, disorientated by the glimmering ceiling, hang suspended upside down. It's not a trip for the novice: the swift undercurrents are unpredictable.

And twenty kilometres farther north, perhaps buried in the sand all these years, you could stumble over a relic from a Portuguese man-o'-war. Vasco da Gama first set foot in East Africa in 1498 at Malindi — having veered away from Mombasa when his anchor ropes were cut — and immediately made friends with the Sultan. By all accounts the Sultan and his predecessors were sociable and cultured. Earlier, in 1417, to the astonishment of the recipient mandarin, they despatched a giraffe to the Emperor of China. Two years later, a fleet arrived with reciprocal gifts — and the Malindi resident who had been sent along to China as Keeper of the Giraffe.

Vasco da Gama's welcome was memorable. 'For nine days we had fetes, sham fights and musical performances.' Finally, loaded with fruit and provisions, the Sultan saw the Portuguese mariners off, sending along with them a local pilot who knew the sea route to Calcutta and thus the sea voyage from Portugal to India was pioneered. Vasco da Gama is remembered by the monument which stands on the headland where he stepped ashore.

The town stands around the sweep of a wide bay — one of the few places along the coast where the reef is broken and the Indian Ocean swell rolls in to make surfboarding possible.

Malindi remained virtually unchanged, apart from a few settler retirement homes and a golf club, until the 1960s when it became the vanguard of the package tour set. Beach hotels sprang up almost overnight and now, along with Swahili and English, German and Italian dialects echo in the colourful markets.

On the south side of the town is Kenya's first marine national park: an

underwater wonderland threatened by the thousands of tons of silt

Above: Coral stone walls of the ruined village of Jumba, near Mtwapa Creek on Kenya's north coast, remained buried by the jungle and undiscovered until the late 1960s.

which wash down the Sabaki each rainy season, destroying the resident tropical fish and the fragile coral structures created over thousands of years.

From the 1930s, ever since author Ernest Hemingway arrived to essay his favourite recreation — only to spend more time tippling gin in the bar of the Blue Marlin than trolling for tunny — Malindi has been the locale for most of Kenya's big game fishing tournaments. From all over the world deep sea sports anglers fly in to joust with the giants for which the Kenya coast is renowned.

For many, however, the essence of this coast is best savoured in the 300 kilometres that stretch north of Malindi, starting almost immediately after you quit the tarmac on the other side of the Sabaki suspension bridge.

At Ngomeni, there's a fascinating juxtaposition between the Arabian Nights ambience of the village — discreet maidens dressed in veils, minarets and castellated mosques — and twentieth-century technology. Out at sea stands the San Marco satellite launching pad, built by the Italians in the 1960s. Fortunately, only rarely do the flaming pyrotechnics of space exploration and weather sensoring light up the night sky. For most of the time it's possible to believe you've taken a step or two back down through the centuries.

Not far inland from Ngomeni, at Marafu, is a weird, strikingly coloured lunar landscape of eroded pinnacles and cliffs, dubbed by locals 'Hell's Kitchen'. And at Gongoni, also notable among the attractions close to Malindi, are man-made lagoons, where the incoming tide is

Above: Pillar marks the spot at Malindi where Vasco da Gama stepped ashore 500 years ago.

Right: Bell tower, Mombasa Island, warned runaway slaves of approaching traders.

Above right: Unique fifteenth-century pillar tomb in front of a Malindi mosque.

Above: Seventeenth-century tomb of the Sheikh of Changwame, whose family were among the original rulers of Mombasa.

trapped and salt recovered by evaporation.

Here you can step out seaward — literally — to experience an incredible dream made real. A European settler family have turned a coral atoll into a castaway Robinson Crusoe island, complete with cordon-bleu seafood and mandatory water sports. At low water you can walk across from the mainland to this desert *pied-à-terre* in ankle-deep water.

To the north of the island stretches the magnificent sweep of Formosa Bay, unprotected by a reef, pounded by breakers which make for enthralling surfing. Kenya's largest river, the Tana, discharges its flow into the bay from a sprawling mangrove swamp delta, which backs up inshore forty kilometres to Garsen, capital of the heartland of the Orma and Pokomo people.

In spate, during exceptional rains, the Tana is an awesome river, often spilling out on either side of its banks for ten kilometres or more. What passes for the main road to Lamu vanishes under the waters or becomes a sea of glutinous mud. The current too swift to risk the perilous passage, the antiquated ferry comes to a standstill on one bank or the other.

But there's no accommodation at Garsen that has pretension to the title of hotel. At such times the Pokomo boatmen do a roaring trade, using their dugout canoes as amphibious versions of the ubiquitous *matatus* which stream along Kenya's many highways. They ferry the waiting tourists, back-packers and local itinerants across to the other side, where little has changed in a thousand years. Seaward, in the tangle of mangrove swamps in the delta, are the remnants of the eccentric enterprises — rubber plantations and such — initiated by the equally eccentric Europeans and locals who settled here around the turn of the century.

In the 1860s the Sultan of Witu cut a canal across the swamps between the Tana and a small stream called Ozi to exploit the Tana waters. Two decades later, in 1892, it engulfed his plantations when the flooded Tana adopted the canal as its avenue and changed course permanently. It still pours into the Indian Ocean at Kipini.

Now forlorn and deserted, save for its small local villages, Witu, with its abundant mango plantations, once prospered. Its end came after the Sultan — an absconder who fled the northern island of Pate in the Lamu archipelago in 1862 when he offended the much more powerful Sultan of Zanzibar — signed an alliance with the brothers Dendhart from Germany in 1888. Known as *Simba*, Swahili for lion, he proclaimed Witu the state of Swahililand — even issuing his own coins and postage stamps.

But the Berlin treaty of 1890 swept aside this puny alliance. Nonetheless, nine Germans planning to establish a sawmill in the princedom stayed on — angering the new Sultan, son of Simba. During an argument, one of the Germans shot his guard and was killed in return, along with the others.

The Sultan refused to discuss this matter with the new administration, so a British expeditionary force of almost one thousand razed the town and surrounding plantations.

There has to be something in the air of this region that induces madness. At least three early colonial officers are reputed to have committed suicide while based at Kipini, where the wreck of the launch

47

Pelican — in which one District Commissioner would fly the British flag as far upstream as Garissa — lay rusting on a mudbank for years.

It was here too, before the First World War, that another European settler — Charlie 'Coconut' Winton — decided to set up a new plantation in Witu. It failed and Winton, retiring to his house in Lamu, closed its doors, never to set foot outside them for forty years.

A contemporary character was Percy Petley, who also experimented disastrously with Witu agriculture — he went bankrupt — and then set up Petley's Inn in Lamu. It acquired a reputation as one of the most eccentric hostelries in the long history of inn-keeping. Surprised guests were often told to cook their own food. If they objected, they were ordered to leave the premises.

Lamu, rather like Gibbon said of Abyssinia, slept in its own shadows 'for nigh on a thousand years, forgetful of the world which was forgetful of it'. The Victorian Europeans must have arrived with something like the impact of Zeus sending down a sudden thunderbolt from the heavens.

For the beat generation of the 1960s, Lamu was at the other end of the rainbow from Freak Street in Kathmandu. In Lamu, all they had to do was drop out as opposed to popping out, on a mixture of hashish and marijuana, in the Nepal capital.

These shaggy-haired wanderers had more to do with bringing the town out of its Rip van Winkle slumbers than the visit of Henry Morton Stanley a century before. Its modern renaissance began when the first of them walked down its narrow alleys and lanes. Outwardly, however,

Above: Wind fills the lateen sails of two dhows, vessels that have traded between Africa and Arabia for more than 2,000 years, as they leave the sheltered waters of Kilifi Creek.

Right: Traditional inshore dhow at low water.

little changed in this strictly Islamic city, where the only motor car —
belonging to the District Officer — can travel little more than two
kilometres, none of it in the built-up area.

The main form of transport and travel is by donkey. There were so
many of these creatures at work in the town in the 1980s that an outraged
citizen — irked by the droppings in the streets — called for the creation of
donkey nappies to keep his fair city clean.

Yet Lamu still retains its air of slumbering mystery. It is the last
survivor of a thousand-year-old civilization that developed between the
ninth and nineteenth centuries. But it was first settled as early as the
second century. The elegant centuries-old houses with their *cortiles*
reflect a heritage that introduced running water plumbing and simple air-
conditioning while Europe was still in bondage to the dark ages.
Occasionally a door leading to one of these flowered courtyards, filled
with fragrant blooms, some with fountains, opens — revealing a blaze of
cool colour within.

In the alleyways sloe-eyed maidens, clad in the all-embracing black
robe — *bui-bui* — that denotes the modesty of their faith, only their eyes
open to public gaze, giggle shyly as they stroll about their domestic
errands.

Like Mombasa and Malindi, Lamu was a thriving port and sultanate in
the sixteenth century, frequently at ritualized war with its neighbours:
Pate, Siyu and Faza, all island kingdoms of this northern archipelago. For
centuries they would sail across, pennants flying, richly uniformed,
orchestrating their battle cries with style and dignity, to taunt their rivals. 49

Actual conflict was well down the list of essential heroics, but when the armies met the end was often bloody.

In 1813 the Nabhani of Pate fatally miscalculated the ebb of the tide when his fleet sailed into Shela, a Lamu beach, to fling down what was probably meant to be a metaphoric gauntlet at the Sultan's feet.

Enraged, the Sultan ordered an advance and the Pate battalions retreated swiftly to their boats — which were now left high and dry by the retreating tide. The result was a grisly massacre from which Lamu emerged the golden winner. All trade was theirs, and they waxed rich for sixty years until the British forced Zanzibar to sign an anti-slaving pact. It brought British naval patrols along the coast to blockade the slave ships, missionaries and crusaders like Stanley, who asserted authority in the Island kingdom. Decline was swift, prosperity only re-emerging with the unlikely advance of the hippies which marked the beginning of Lamu's golden age as a tourist resort.

Unaffected by these momentous influences, and perhaps content to be so, Siyu and Pate gaze across the creek at their prosperous neighbour. Siyu's stout fort and rusting cannon, recalling the more violent past, now offers only a placid mirror image on the glassy calm of the unruffled surface of the backwater of forgotten history to which fate has consigned it.

A grass landing strip carved out of the tropical forest is all that denotes Pate's place in the twentieth century. Donkeys carry the rare visitor through jungle trail, mango and coconut plantations, across its unspoilt 50 hinterland, pausing briefly in their passage through thatched villages,

Above: Shela Beach, Lamu — scene of a grisly massacre when a rival Sultan's army were left high and dry by the retreating tide.

Above: Dhows and boats line Lamu's ancient waterfront.

crowded with laughing girls and stern-visaged menfolk, to the recently uncovered ruins of the oldest known settlement on the coast.

Serious excavation on the lost city of Shanga began in 1980 when an Operation Drake team, led by archaeologist Mark Horton, dug down through several layers of houses and streets to its ninth-century level. The dry fossils and ancient ruins they found there reveal the bare bones of a fascinating flesh-and-blood drama covering several centuries. High-class merchants and their women lived lives of splendour in this busy port-state until, centuries after it was established, the retreating sea left it high and dry.

Now only the echoes of its past haunt the eight hectares of ruins, some with recesses where ceramics and works of art were displayed. The mosque, with its *kiblah* pointing east to Mecca, denotes the prevailing faith, but slowly the inhabitants left — leaving only the legacy of a graceful age. It's a vivid contrast to the cultures inland on the mainland, which they plundered for slaves and artefacts as the source of their wealth.

A hundred kilometres north of Pate lies a string of uninhabited coral islands save for a thatched tourist village on Kiwaiyu Island, truly the most 'away-from-it-all' retreat of any in Kenya. Pounding surf undercuts the seaward side of these islands where, astonishingly, bushbuck, monkeys, porcupines, and wild pigs roam on the ground; counterpoint to the cry of the wild birds nesting in the cliffs.

An old colonial officer's house stands on the mainland at Kiunga, a lotus-eating village shrouded in palms — sole evidence of Britain's

51

In 1896, when the first spur of the Uganda Railway began to arrow out of Mombasa, daily the tides surged up Kilindini Creek into a narrow bottleneck, separating the island from the mainland. George Whitehouse, the general manager, bridged this gap with a timber viaduct. Today an earth causeway carries the metre-gauge track across to the mainland. Technically, Mombasa is an island no more.

Yet the panorama and leisurely pace remain much the same as that enjoyed by the first settlers and tourists just after the turn of the century when they disembarked from the liners at the docks and boarded the train for the journey upcountry.

Few railways in the world can equal the romance and sense of adventure experienced on the overnight 'express' which leaves the steamy coast before sundown and arrives next morning after sunup in the crisp highland air of Nairobi, 500 kilometres away.

In 1901 the journey could take as long as a week, the ancient locomotives — second-hand rolling stock from India — labouring out of the coastal plain and up the steep slopes of the first escarpment through the Mazeras 'snake', a coil of track which loops around upon itself. In those days it cut close by the mission stations, established in the middle of the last century at Rabai and Ribe by two Lutheran pastors, Johann L. Krapf and his compatriot, Johannes Rebmann. It was Rebmann, during a trip upcountry armed only with a brolly and Bible, who on 11 May 1848 became the first European to see the snows of Kilimanjaro. It was his reports of snow so close to the Equator that first aroused European interest in Kenya.

The train crests the brow of this first plateau, which continues to rise gently inland for 200 kilometres, at Mariakani, where the lush tropical foliage of the coast begins to thin out into scrub bush dotted with occasional palm groves.

Gazing out on this seemingly impenetrable mass of thicket and thorn from the comfort of a railway coach, it's chastening to imagine the young Scotsman, Joseph Thomson, leading his small army of porters through it in 1883. Even by the standards of his more famous contemporaries, Stanley, Livingstone and Speke, he was one of the most extraordinary men ever to penetrate Africa.

Beyond the scrub, the railway spans the treacherous Taru Desert, a scorched wilderness, entirely without water, which is prelude to the daunting but ever-beautiful land and adventure ahead.

The main settlement in the Taru is Mackinnon Road, another memorial to the unfulfilled sense of mission of that prudent Victorian. Ahead of his grandiose Central African Railway he sent a construction team, including Sergeant George Ellis of the Royal Engineers, under Captain Sclater, which cut a trail in Thomson's footsteps along the line taken later by the rail surveyors.

The actual road followed roughly the line of the caravan trail to Lake Victoria and through Fort Smith on the eastern shoulders of the Rift Valley Escarpment. It was intended to accomplish what was finally left to the Railway to achieve: open up the interior for profitable trading. In the event, for many years after the Railway came into existence, it did sterling service. Even at Independence, motorists still travelled much of the way from Mombasa to Nairobi along this dirt road: tarmac was not

Preceding pages: Hot-air balloon carrying entranced tourists drifts over the Kenya savannah as a herd of impala take flight.

Above: An endless vista of plains and mountains stretches as far as the eye can see from the 7,000-foot-high crest of the evergreen Taita Hills in south-east Kenya.

completed until 1969.

On either side lies unspoilt Kenya — north, in the direction of Somalia, lies the great arid hinterland sparsely peopled by hardy nomadic stock; to the south, in the direction of Tanzania, lies the savannah inhabited mainly by the great plains game of Africa.

A minority of these nomads are the Watu, perhaps Kenya's oldest original inhabitants, descendants of ethnic groups which lived here thousands of years ago. They speak a language which has affinities with the click-speaking Bushmen of the Kalahari and Okavango of southern Africa. More similarities arise in the bush lore they display.

Today, numbering only around 5,000, the Watu's traditional economy is based on hunting and gathering. Watching the women of the related Boni group following the rains, digging for roots, berries and fruits, is to witness a pattern of resourcefulness and resilience which enables these communities to survive natural disaster after natural disaster. Even the stems of wild plants, chopped up, provide a valuable source of nourishment during drought and famine. The pith is fermented, washed in hot water and ground into flour to make a sustaining porridge.

The Watu are Kenya's most renowned trackers and hunters. Hundreds of years before the archers of Plantagent England faced the French at Agincourt, they were using the long bow. Though strictly against the law, even today they use these weapons to pursue elephants, not as mercenary poachers, but in search of meat outside the periphery — and sometimes within it — of the long reaches of Tsavo East National Park.

Together with Tsavo West, this was one of Kenya's original National

57

almost entirely on the dexterity, flexibility and strength of that astonishing appendage, an elongated nose, their trunk. They also use it for scent, communication, washing, carrying and clearing. The tusks are simply secondary — but important — lifting, carrying and clearing tools.

These days the tusks of males seldom exceed forty-five kilograms each. The heaviest on record — taken in the Kilimanjaro region — weighed 103 kilograms and the longest, measured on the curve, was close to four metres. Gregarious and highly social animals, they respond to touch and, apart from mankind, are the only creatures that bury their dead. They live in herds ranging in size from twenty to one thousand.

An eighty-five-hectare man-made dam at Aruba inside the waterless Taru Desert, some forty kilometres from the clifftop lookout, staunches the seasonal flow of the Voi River off the Taita Hills, in the south-west, and provides a large reservoir for elephant and plains game. Visitors camp here in a style reminiscent, but much more secure and comfortable, of early adventurers like Thomson.

Much of Tsavo East is inaccessible to the public, but those areas that are open evoke memories of the grandeur which was Africa's. A private

Above: Young elephant, calf resting in its shadows, enjoys a dust bath using its trunk as a spray.

Above: Tusks and trunks intertwined, two young elephants in playful mood in Amboseli National Park. Elephant tusks are used for clearing, feeding and carrying.

wildlife reserve adjoining the park, spread over 250,000 hectares, maintains a valuable nucleus of breeding herds of rare species and an esoteric safari experience. The Galana Game Ranch hosts costly, tailor-made stays in the bush for a wealthy elite.

The ranch lies under the lea of the 300-kilometre-long Yatta Plateau. One of the world's longest lava flows, the plateau overshadows the Athi-Galana River, spawned in the Ngong Hills close to Nairobi, for much of the river's course. Near Galana, the river, mighty when in spate, cascades over Lugard's Falls through a narrow neck. Brave or foolhardy as you may be, it's said you can stand astride the top of the falls and watch the waters plunge down to the pool below, where crocodiles bask motionless in the sun. The falls are named after Lord Lugard, Britain's first proconsul in East Africa.

South of Voi, the rugged Taita Hills — seen from a distance as a bulking mass of blue-grey rock — thrust into the white clouds that sail across the sky. Closer to they take on a more gentle aspect, like a verdant island rising out of the savannah ocean. Some of this grassland is turned over to sisal production, but much is marginal, preserving an unspoilt

61

Left: Maasai giraffe lopes across the Amboseli plains beneath Kilimanjaro, at right of picture.

Overleaf: Three lioness gorge themselves on a wildebeest kill.

wilderness for a wildlife spectacle that has its equal only in Kenya's and Tanzania's other large game sanctuaries.

For bird lovers, the prime attraction is Lake Jipe astride the Kenya-Tanzania border, its reed beds and dappled waters set against the background of the Pare Mountains where, from small villages, slender spirals of smoke climb unwavering into the still air. You can hire a punt from the National Park office on its shores to explore its waters.

Floating on the lake — perhaps in Tanzanian waters, for nothing marks the division between one nation and the other — watching the sudden swoop of a cormorant as it dives beneath the surface for a fish, is euphoric. All life hangs motionless, caught in a frozen moment of eternity.

There's a baroque monument nearby, however, that testifies to the brevity of life and the strength of man's conceit — a many-bedroomed castle, with the dimensions and perspectives of a medieval European fortress. It's known hereabouts as Grogan's Folly, built by Ewart Grogan, the man who walked from the Cape to Cairo for love of a woman. He settled in Kenya like a latter-day Rhodes to build himself a fortune, often without scruple.

Just a short drive up the road from its gates is the border town of Taveta. In 1924 it was linked to the main railway line, and today there's a twice-weekly train — on Wednesdays and Saturdays — from Voi to this bustling market town. When built, it was extended across the border to Moshi to join up with the Tanzanian Railway system, and later merged with the Uganda and Tanganyika railway systems as the East African Railways. The link was broken in the 1970s when a section of track just out of Taveta was pulled up, but it was restored later in the 1980s.

Taveta and the surrounding region was the only theatre of war in Africa during the First World War, when Tanganyika was a German colony. Taveta fell into German hands when their forces attacked the town on 15 August 1914 — just eleven days after the outbreak of war. Nine days after Taveta was evacuated, a patrol, led astray by inaccurate British maps, was captured on the stretch between Voi and Sultan Hamud.

For the next four years the Taveta region was a focal point of the conflict in East Africa and inspired one of the great epics of military history. The main railway line in Kenya was a strategic target for the Germans, who sent out marauders from Taveta.

When the Germans retreated, a small remnant force of German and African soldiers, led by Colonel Lettow von Worbeck, continued to harass the much stronger British forces — only retreating when challenged by an expeditionary force numbering more than 200,000 under the command of General Jan Smuts — in a series of hit-and-run raids. This epic formed the theme of Wilbur Smith's book *Shout at the Devil*, later made into a movie.

It's commemorated today in a game lodge built, out of sandbags cemented together, in the style of a German fort alongside the Voi-Taveta line, part of a private 11,000-hectare game reserve operated by the Hilton International group. Its sister lodge reflects a more African ambience, a series of rondavels raised on concrete stilts and connected by walkways, beneath which large herds of elephant browse, undisturbed by the

63

intrusive tourists.

You can stand on these in the breathless still of an indigo African night, the stars above like diamonds in the sky, and by the luminous light of a tropical moon watch the shadowy bulk of an elephant as it ambles slowly beneath, munching fodder as it pauses, one of a herd of perhaps a hundred or more making their way in their own time to the salt lick and waterhole in front of the lodge.

Set in an unfenced wildlife wilderness, these are probably the most unusual conference centres in the world: where tycoons, business magnates and top executives meet, surrounded by lion, elephant, buffalo and countless other species.

In effect, the game sanctuary in which the properties stand is an extension of the vast Tsavo National Park. Virtually every major species of Kenyan wildlife finds a home here, save the reserve's three rhinoceros. This imperilled species, hunted ruthlessly for its worthless horn — valued at US$25,000 a pound for its supposedly curative properties — has been mown down from 20,000 animals in 1970 to fewer than 500.

In 1986 game wardens feared so much for the safety of Salt Lick's resident rhinos that they drugged them with tranquilizing darts. They were then captured and relocated among a protected breeding nucleus in the lea of the Ngulia Hills, not far away in Tsavo West.

Typical of Salt Lick's natural theatre was the day ten lionesses, some fully grown cubs, others mothers training them to hunt, stalked to the outlying waterhole around noon and lurked within the tall grasses

Above: Halo of clouds encircles Kibo, the 19,340-foot-high ice-cap of Africa's highest mountain, Kilimanjaro, with the sister peak of Mawenzi at right looking down on the rippled waters of euphorbia-framed Lake Chala.

fringing its banks as hordes of zebra, water buck, impala and hartebeeste gave yelps, barks and snorts of alarm.

Disdainfully, from the distant gallery forests of the dry rivers to the east and south, always feeding as they moved, came phalanxes of elephant, different herds numbering collectively close to a thousand beasts, each herd following its own sure trail to Salt Lick's ever-abundant waterhole; in dry times the only source of liquid for many kilometres around.

One herd, including a mother with a two-day-old calf, came close to the pride of lioness. Carefully, the mother guided its toddler underneath her protective bosom as the lionesses stalked nearer. Ears flapping forward and then back against the neck, she charged — sending the predators scattering. Some lurked, hidden behind the bush. Still the vigilant mother did not relax her guard, seeking out each until, almost shamefaced, the last great cat slunk away in dejection.

Lion, accustomed to coveys of ubiquitous safari vehicles, gather in large and gregarious groups, lolling in the sun. Swift and dangerous, these creatures present a contradictory demeanour to most onlookers: rarely moving and looking on the hordes who have saved for years to experience Africa in the wild with amber-eyed indifference.

Weighing up to 280 kilograms, unmistakable in size and majesty, lion are the largest of the three great cats which roam Kenya. Their circular eyes, like those of the leopard, differ from the oval-shaped eyes of most cats. Lion are prodigious jumpers — able to clear a four-metre-high hurdle or twelve-metre-wide chasm. They hunt communally. The favourite method is to pounce on a victim's back, dragging it to the ground and seizing it by the throat. Another method is suffocation: the lion will hold the victim's muzzle in its mouth. An individual lion kills on average nineteen head of game a year at an average weight of about 114 kilograms for each kill. A lion or lioness can wolf down as much as twenty-five kilograms of flesh in a sustained orgy of eating, thereafter going without food for as long as five days.

Wherever you go in this volcanic landscape, grassed over with savannah and scrub and thorn, the rugged 7,000-foot-high Taita Hills — an upthrust of rocky spires, great bluffs and massive whale back peaks — dominate the view. And, far-distant to the south-west, the flat ice-cap of Africa's greatest mountain, 19,340-foot-high Kilimanjaro, floats above a halo of cloud, remote from Salt Lick's scorching plains at 2,000 feet above sea level.

Craggy and forbidding in appearance, the Hills in fact hold within their embrace a series of *Shangri-la*-like valleys bountiful in their harvests of fruit, vegetables and flowers. The road winds up to Wundanyi in a series of tortuous hairpin bends. Within twenty minutes Africa is remote and distant. The smallholdings and neat terraces which step down the steep sides of the hills could be in the Mediterranean. Only the farmers and their families remind you that this is the other side of the world.

The Taita-Taveta people were among the first inland Kenyans with whom the missionaries and Thomson made contact. Divided into seven clans, they have long farmed the land: always with a a great many spiritual preliminaries. Cultivation requires authority from the tribal elders and sacrifices and supplications made to the collections of skulls,

Above: Treebound cheetah studies the Amboseli
National Park grasslands for potential prey, beneath
Kilimanjaro's majestic peak.

kept in sacred caves, which contain the ancestral spirits. Proud, hard-working and full of character, the Taita have made a large contribution to development since Independence, through an elite cadre of dedicated civil and private executives and politicians.

Many also practise fishing: in Lake Jipe and the gem-like Lake Chala which lies hidden, above Taveta town, on the slopes of Kilimanjaro — again divided in half by the invisible Kenya-Tanzania border. One hundred metres deep, fed by the melting snows of Africa's greatest mountain percolating deep underground, one of the mysteries of this lake — which lies within a steep-sided volcanic crater — are the resident Nile crocodile. How they came to exist here nobody knows.

In the main, however, Tsavo West, once thickly wooded, has been transformed over the years into open grass and bushland by the great herds of elephant roaming endlessly across its red earth, victim of the occasional savage drought that turns the park into a dust-bowl.

Yet, by the late 1980s, good, consistent rains and a reduction in the number of elephants had regenerated Tsavo's woodlands, yet another revolution in the ageless cycle of nature.

At the park's centre, a range of sheer cliffs, the Ngulia Hills rise out of the plains 2,000 feet below. A lodge was built atop these cliffs in 1970 and has created a great avian phenomenon. In October and November during the short rains, when mists are frequent, millions of migrating birds make their passage southward over this region of Kenya. Disorientated by the shadowy glow of the lodge's artificial moon, they come down low in their thousands — enabling ornithologists to net and ring them. Thus, many secrets of the immense distances that these birds navigate with uncanny instinct have been revealed.

The seasonal Tsavo River flows around the base of the Ngulia and a few kilometres north-eastward, where it's bridged by the main Mombasa-Nairobi line, there's an incongruously modern motel called the Maneaters. Nothing indicates, however, that this was the location of one of the epic dramas of Victorian railroad construction.

When R. O. Preston established the railhead on this spot in mid-1898 he thought it would only be a matter of days before moving on. The resident wildlife thought differently.

Two lions held several thousand Indian and more than 1,300 African workers at bay in a siege that lasted for weeks. Several Africans and almost thirty Indians were killed by these shadowy man-eaters in a stranger-than-fiction scenario that became an epic story of suspense and terror, later related by Colonel J. H. Patterson in the book, *Man Eaters of Tsavo*. This military martinet, the self-appointed saviour of the fear-crazed rail gangs, bungled ambush after ambush, but finally despatched the two killers and then glorified his role by writing a best seller that captured the imagination of Victorian Britain.

While all this was going on, Preston had floated himself and his advance party across the river and moved relentlessly on towards the half-way stage, Mtito Andei, still little more than a sleepy halt in the desert. Beside the rail station, there are three or four service stations and cafeterias and a once plush hotel. But Mtito Andei serves its purpose as the main gateway into Tsavo West on one side and Tsavo East on the other.

There's an abundance of wonders in both sections. Not too far from Mtito Andei, along Tsavo West's well-kept network of red dirt roads, is a clump of acacia and doum palms that rings Mzima Springs, a fount of cool, clear water. One hundred kilometres distant, the Equatorial sun melts the snow peak of 19,340-foot-high Kilimanjaro. The water filters down thousands of feet through the mountain's volcanic strata, to flow deep underground and join up with underground rivers flowing from the nearby Chyulu Hills, to burst out in Mzima Springs at a peak rate of almost 500 million litres a day.

Years ago a film team constructed an underwater observation post in the banks of the Springs. Clamber down a few steps and you enter a new world: hippo move across the bed of the springs in stately slow motion, rather like moon walkers. Fat tilapia swim by slowly in great schools. No anglers lure them to the hook or net here — only the sudden swirl of a Nile crocodile gliding through the water controls their numbers. Mzima's bounty does not end there.

Until the 1980s, the springs were Mombasa's sole source of water, sent gushing down the 150-kilometre-long pipeline, now supplemented by a scheme that draws its supplies from the Sabaki at Malindi. In sultry Mombasa there's always a moment to savour the incongruity — and pleasure — of drinking water drawn from the frozen heights of Africa's highest mountain.

South-west of Mzima is the first wildlife lodge built in a Kenya national park, Kilaguni, opened in 1962 by the Duke of Gloucester. It was inspiration for the host of others that followed in wildlife sanctuaries

across the country and fulfilment of a concept that harnesses the work of conservation to that of tourist attraction. Reflections of Kilimanjaro in a salmon-pink sundown sky float on the still surface of a water-hole, until jarred by the ripple of a herd of zebra come to drink.

Nothing in Africa's great panoramas surpasses the matchless majesty of Kilimanjaro. All through 1897 and 1898, Preston and his gangs woke each day at the crack of dawn and gazed in brief wonder at this distant spectacle floating above the hot and arid plains 100 kilometres away. As they climbed the gentle gradient north-westward to the Rift, it was always visible on the south-western horizon, except during the rainy season.

From Mtito Andei, the arid boundary of the land of the Wakamba, the railway line pushed on to Kibwezi, a dark and sombre place where malaria and blackwater fever were endemic. But prolonged drought, while hastening the famine that swept the area, made conditions bearable.

Next, the line wound on towards Mile 200, somewhere near Makindu, where a Sikh samaritan temple now stands — offering haven for the weary traveller free of charge: a living example of the tenets of the Guru Nanak faith. Not far from the temple is Hunter's Lodge, named after the man who built a small safari lodge on the site — one of Kenya's great

Above: Prodigious lovers, lion and lioness rest little when mating — the act occurring as often as 300 times in the course of a single week.

Above: Lioness feed on carcass. On average, a full-grown lion accounts for nineteen head of game a year, wolfing down as much as twenty-five kilos of meat in one sustained orgy of feasting.

white hunters, J. J. Hunter, a Scotsman, who in this area alone killed more than a thousand rhinoceros on a government contract.

But rhino then numbered tens of thousands. Hunter may well have begun their decline and fall. Less than a century later, in 1987, Kenya's entire rhino population had been so decimated game officials would have felt themselves lucky to count just the number that Hunter slew.

The lodge stands in the northern lea of the 7,000-foot-high Chyulu Hills, surely the jewel in the Tsavo crown, which only four or five centuries ago burst out of the northern edge of the savannah, midway between Tsavo and Amboseli, in an awesome eruption. These are among the world's youngest mountains, arching their narrow back in an eighty-kilometre-long east-to-west ridge. The soil is still harsh and gritty lava, coated occasionally, after the brief rains, with a veneer of fragile grass. Deep beneath is a catacomb of eerie caves, some stretching more than twelve kilometres, many perhaps longer but still unexplored.

A dirt road climbs through the scrub thorn and acacia in a series of zig-zag bends and up through stunted forest and saplings to the open grassy ridge at the top. From the southern crest of the hills, the shimmering plains stretch away to Amboseli National Park and the foot of Kilimanjaro. After the last spasm of eruptions which formed the Chyulu Hills faded, a trickle of molten lava rolled out from its feet across

the plains. Today the traveller from Tsavo to Amboseli crosses this coagulated tar-like barrier, named after the Devil, *Shaitani*, by the superstitious locals who lived in this wild region in those days.

By early 1899 the railhead had passed the northern extremity of the Chyulu and reached Mile 250 at the base of the second great inland steppe, the foothills of the Ukambani range, which rise steeply between 1,500 and 2,000 feet to level out into the Kapiti and Athi plains. It had passed through a place known as *Simba*, the Swahili word for lion, where the bush was infested with this King of Beasts, and Emali, and now rested in the shadows of a gaunt outcrop that rose up sheer out of the land.

It was here then, with some pomp and circumstance, that the ruler of Zanzibar arrived to inspect the progress of this curious British enterprise. The town already springing up around the railhead was duly christened Sultan Hamud in his honour, and so it remains.

There was peril — and breathtaking beauty — around every bend and atop every hill. South-east lay the dusty alluvial Maasai Plains. A spur line branched out into this wilderness to a dot on the map called Kibini where rail engineers sank a borehole to tap the waters of Kilimanjaro and slake the voracious thirst of the steeds of steam and fire which hauled the railway lines and platelayers remorselessly forward. Much later the line was upgraded for wagons to move rock quarried for the cement factory at Athi River.

Now began the testing climb with its severe gradients up to the next steppe — through Kima, which a year later was to earn a notoriety almost as great as that of the Tsavo bridge. In June 1900, another man-eater ambushed its ambusher — Charles Ryall, a young inspector on attachment from the Indian police to the Uganda Railway police — as he lay in wait for it inside a sleeping coach. His body is buried in the little cemetery at the end of the Railway Golf Course on Nairobi's Uhuru Highway, a stone's throw from the Nairobi Railway Museum, where the

Above left: Traders prepare for the day's business at colourful Tala Market near Machakos in Kambaland.

Above: Young warrior about to join ranks of the Maasai elders. His mother and friends ritually shave his coiffeur.

Opposite: Young Maasai girl is crowned with tiara of brightly-coloured beads following circumcision.

72

coach in which it all happened is a star exhibit.

And then it was up through Ulu and over the crest of the Ukambanis to Konza, which was as far south as the line would ever reach (though many since have wished it would venture south forever) over the Kapiti Plains between Kilimanjaro and the Ngong Hills, a ridge of knuckles lying — a vague blue-grey — on the distant south-west horizon. For where the plains rolled away — into infinity it seemed — was a sight that drew the breath of all who saw it.

It was a spectacle that so aroused ex-US President Teddy Roosevelt that, groping for the superlative superlative, he called it the Pleistocene Age of Animals. At that time these plains formed part of the 25,000 square kilometres of the Great Southern Game reserve. Mile after mile of savannah was a living blur of creatures, a mass so solid the species were sometimes indistinct — thousands upon thousands of antelope and gazelle, lofty giraffe, menacing rhinoceros, stealthy lion and the cheetah's fluid grace. It also enraptured Winston Churchill, who stopped the train, like so many settlers, and while it waited by some small halt went hunting.

Kilimanjaro now lay south-east, some 150 kilometres away. In the hot dry season from December to March it was clearly visible from Konza. Ringed still by a halo of clouds, its wedding cake peak floats disembodied in the clear African sky but no phantom ever had such substance as this massive piece of natural masonry spewed up a million years ago in a great eruption and still steaming. It's the highest free-standing mountain in the world, and one of the greatest volcanoes ever to burst through the earth's crust.

Thirteen years after Rebmann first saw Kilimanjaro, a German — Baron Klaus von der Decken — climbed 14,000 feet up the mountain and experienced a providential fall of snow. But it was a British missionary to Kenya who became the first known European to explore these eternal snows so close to the Equator. In 1867, the Reverend Charles New laboured beyond the snow level — feared by the Chagga people of the mountain as the abode of vengeful spirits, who were to be disturbed only at the peril of the intruder.

Tanzania is possessively jealous of its great natural wonder, for the views from Kenya on its eastern side, particularly those in Amboseli, which is around 4,000 feet above sea level, are arguably the most dramatic. The mountain rises suddenly from its base 15,000 feet into the sky. A Tanzanian MP once suggested the country's Public Works Department should build a huge wall around the mountain's eastern slopes, cutting out this view, and so encourage tourists to visit Tanzania to see Kilimanjaro.

Kilimanjaro's highest point is Uhuru Peak on the main summit, Kibo. Five kilometres separates this from the saw-toothed peak of Mawenzi, which at 16,890 feet is the third highest point — after Kilimanjaro and Mount Kenya — in Africa.

The mountain, which contains a fifth of all the ice in Africa, is a world in microcosm: from Equatorial tropics, through rain forest, savannah and across true desert — at 15,000 feet — to its permanent ice-cap. Yet the miracle is that once over the lip of 18,740-foot-high Gillman Point on the rim of Kibo's crater, you can look down and see the black lava rock walls

Above: Bat-eared fox, sensitive sonar system ever-alert, outside its den. The ears act as a defence mechanism and also locate the insects on which it feeds.

Above: Leopard feasts on a kill cached in the branches of a euphorbia tree.

of the fumaroles deep inside which still emit steam; thus melting the ice and snow around them.

Strong winds gust permanently at this height, clutching at the sleeves of your windjacket, threatening to tear you off the face of the mountain. Though climbing Kilimanjaro is mainly a laborious, lung-sapping walk for most of the distance, the last 3,000 feet is up a steep scree face that tests both nerve and stamina. Its south and south-western faces, however, offer climbing challenges on ice cliffs and glaciers that capture the imagination of the finest mountaineers in the world.

In 1978, Reinhold Messner, the world's greatest climber, spent several weeks living on the south face, acclimatizing himself for his first attempt on Everest — 9,688 feet higher than Kilimanjaro — and conquered the 5,000-foot Breach Wall of Kibo, dominated by a huge spectacular icicle hanging from the Diamond Glacier.

From Amboseli, however, Kilimanjaro rises up like a gigantic iced cake, always serene and tranquil, cotton-wool clouds scudding across the startling blue of the African sky, a herd of giraffe in the foreground cropping the topmost leaves of an acacia thorn. These images, and the mystery that shrouds the peak, inspired Ernest Hemingway's classic, *The Snows of Kilimanjaro*.

Long before 380 square kilometres of this pristine wilderness were declared a national park, the Nobel laureate delighted in Amboseli's untouched beauty. His enthusiasm fired contemporaries like Robert Ruark and Hollywood film makers. The park, one of Kenya's earliest game sanctuaries, is still a favourite of the movie men.

A Paramount crew, filming a 1948 epic, endowed it with its first lodge. When shooting was finished, the cottages in which the stars, including Ava Gardner, lived were handed over to the local council, who turned the film village into the Ol Tukai self-service lodge for nature and adventure buffs. It still flourishes.

A large area of the park is the alluvial dried-up bed of a seasonal lake and during the dry season the shimmering heat creates a series of mirages. Amboseli is justly famed for its wildlife spectacle. Great herds of elephant and buffalo roam its fragile grasslands and extensive swamps.

Harmony exists between such creatures as these and the Maasai, whose traditional grazing grounds are within this area. Now, ironically, modern development is restricting the land available to both.

The Maasai are a race of warrior pastoralists who moved southward through Africa for the last thousand years, reaching north-east Kenya four or five centuries ago, and arriving in central and southern Kenya and northern Tanzania sometime in the last century.

Above: Weighing more than a ton, the black rhinoceros is now in the last vestiges of existence — down from 20,000 at the beginning of the 1970s to fewer than 500 at the close of the 1980s.

Top: Rare survivor of Kenya's imperilled rhino population frolics in a mud bath in a national park.

There are about 250,000 Kenya Maasai, slowly being swept into the mainstream of national development, despite their reactionary stance to change. Proud, aloof from other societies and cultures, these iconoclastic people are renowned as Africa's most fearsome warriors: with traditions and strategy that bear a marked resemblance to those of the old Roman legions. So does their mien. Lithe and slender, adorned with an ostrich feather or lion mane head-dress, skin oiled and glistening, draped with the loose robe of an ochre-coloured *shuka*, holding their spear, the warriors stand on one leg, the other resting behind their spear. The Maasai warrior, *moran*, is the epitome of military nobility. These aristocratic dandies are possessed of a fine conceit: peacock-proud about their coiffure, a braid of ringlets slicked down with a 'Brylcreem' of muddy ochre. Cattle-herding is not their duty, defence is.

They live by their cattle. Traditionally, tilling the ground and planting is beneath their dignity: cattle represent wealth, status and security. But now, when the grazing is barren, they cannot move their herds on to fresh grounds. On one side a national border restricts their movement southward; on the other sides, farms, smallholdings and development bar the way.

Slowly the Maasai are embracing the national ethic and beginning to make a positive contribution to Kenya's development. New schools are springing up everywhere, and the 1980s initiation ceremonies — circumcision for the elevation to manhood, and *eunoto* for the elevation from warrior to junior elder — were possibly the last of the rites which have been practised faithfully down the millenniums. Circumcision demands a show of passive bravery by the initiate. If he flinches or murmurs when, without anaesthetic, the circumciser cuts the foreskin, 77

Above: Though born with eyes wide open and teeth already cut, hyaena cubs suckle longer than almost any of Africa's wild animals despite eating meat fairly soon after birth. The young are at risk to adults, who often eat them.

Right: Ruthless and efficient hunters as well as notorious scavengers, hyaenas are noted for the wide range of their diet. They eat almost anything — wolfing down even old boots, broomsticks and tin cans.

Above: Wary of larger predators and scavengers, alert jackal feeds off a zebra carcass as an expectant army of vultures and marabou stork wait, ready to move in at the first opportunity.

he will remain a social leper within Maasai society for the rest of his life.

The Maasai display a remarkably liberal attitude towards sexual relations. Warriors cannot marry but are allowed mistresses. When they are elevated to junior elder, they become eligible to marry. Symbolically, wives are regarded as married to all members of an age-group and unwed members may seduce a blood brother's wife. It's not encouraged, but neither is it condemned. The custom has some charm. The age-mate signals his presence by planting his spear outside the matrimonial hut, a notice to the husband and the others that denotes they should not enter — rather like a 'Do Not Disturb' notice on a hotel door.

Inside the hut, the suitor states his case in lyrical language. The initial stage is without contact. They lie on the bed untouching as the man talks in a flurry of romantic images designed to soften the woman's heart. Only if he expresses his ardour articulately enough, will the wife succumb to his embrace.

They live in temporary villages, *enkangs*, in low, dome-shaped houses built of cow dung and wattle. When they move on with the herds, the villages are abandoned.

One of the traditional tests of bravery for newly-elevated warriors is the lion hunt: armed only with a spear and shield. Even today, some young Maasai proudly display the savage scars earned in face-to-face confrontation with these beasts.

For the Maasai, Konza was the north-eastern extremity of their range. Beyond, as far as Kitui and Mwingi, was Kamba country, large areas of it drought prone. Skilled hunters and good agriculturalists, the Kamba also 79

had the relief of highlands, like the Ukumbani and Mua hills. The 'capital', Machakos, a corruption of the name of Masaku, their nineteenth-century diviner and seer, lay in the bowl of a valley ringed by rich and fertile hills.

It was so delightful and so reminiscent of English hill country, with a much more benign climate, that Britain's first administrator in upcountry Kenya, Manchester-born John Ainsworth, at once made it the seat of his administration; building there — in 1894, long before the railway — a substantial fort and compound from which to oversee his extremely large parish. He was confident that when railhead arrived, it would become the commercial as well as administrative capital of the central highlands.

In the north of Kambaland lies the rounded dome of Kilimambogo, the Mountain of the Buffalo. In the pleasant hills between the now rich coffee farms and smallholdings is the farm town of Kagundo, a rural suburb of Nairobi, delightful in its contrasts with that bustling city, and the colourful Tala market, a blaze of riotous colours and jostle of thrifty hard-working farmers and traders.

The Maasai occupied the rangelands south of Konza well into Tanzania, beyond Namanga, which is the border town between the two countries and stands at the eastern foot of 8,287-foot-high Ol Doinyo Orok — the Black Mountain.

In the south-west, these vast plains end abruptly on the lip of the eastern escarpment of the Great Rift Valley, which first became known as a result of John Walter Gregory's work in the 1890s. Not long after Thomson trekked through these same lands, this young Scottish geologist made his way upcountry to investigate this awesome flaw in the earth's surface. Clearly visible 90,000 kilometres out in space, the Rift stretches for more than 5,000 kilometres — from Lake Bailak in Russia, across Jordan, down the Red Sea and south down to Beira in Mozambique.

Nowhere is it more dramatic or scenically picturesque than in Kenya,

Above: Lion mate with obsessive compulsion. One couple were recorded copulating 360 times in one week.

Above: Hundreds of wildebeest mingle at water's edge with their constant companions, the zebra. During the yearly migration to the Maasai Mara the honking, braying calls and dust raised by their hooves fills the air.

Overleaf: Unequalled as a natural spectacle, the Maasai Mara's yearly migration of wildebeest number more than 1.5 million creatures — along with large herds of zebra and other antelope and crowds of ever-attendant predators.

where it plunges more than 5,000 feet in places, with a width of up to 100 kilometres between its eastern and western walls. Gregory travelled as far north as Baringo, where he hammered out samples of rock strata from different levels in the escarpment walls and returned to Britain to proclaim his theory of how the Rift was created.

Earlier in his travels, he came across the Rift on his approach from the Kapiti Plains, which descend more gently to the Valley floor than in many places, with the Meto Hills — of which the Black Mountain is the most dominant peak — forming the Valley's eastern flank.

Descending the various faults, Gregory stumbled over a clearing on the rocky plain above Magadi littered with bones. Thirty years later, that indefatigible fossil hunter, Dr Louis Leakey, *enfant terrible* of archaeology, who dedicated his life to the search for mankind's origins, cleared the site. There, on the ground all around, lay dramatic evidence of the first creature to abandon a four-legged posture and walk upright.

Our earliest ancestor, *Homo erectus*, who took his first faltering footsteps on the shores of Lake Turkana in Kenya's north, had quickly become an adept pedestrian. Groups had moved south and lived around Olorgasailie, where they had hunted. The fossils on the ground were the broken skeletons of a race of giant baboons long extinct. They had been slain by rough weapons of chipped stones and crude cobbles that also lay around — fashioned of rock that does not occur naturally in this part of the Rift. Man had become a hunter. You can see the fossils today — a tenuous thread in the still tangled and yet to be unravelled tapestry of the story of mankind.

Gregory also discovered one of the world's greatest deposits of soda: Lake Magadi, the second largest single source — after California's Salton Sea in the USA — in the world.

The lake's 100 square kilometres form a drainage sump without an outlet. Set only 1,900 feet above sea level, the sun's rays funnel mercilessly into this arena, and the intense evaporation creates ideal conditions for excavating the trona for only in rare rains is the lake covered with water. Mineral rights were granted by the British to two prospectors, Deacon and Walsh, who staked a claim to Magadi in 1901.

In September 1911, the company that was established as a result, signed a contract with George Pauling to build a 150-kilometre-long railway line from Konza to Magadi. It passes through Kajiado, the pleasant administrative centre of Kenya's southernmost Maasai — and within twenty-five kilometres of Olorgesailie — as it winds its way down to the scorched floor of the Great Rift Valley: a Dante's inferno of lava boulders and craggy tors, frequently smouldering in temperatures of more than 110° Farenheit.

From Kajiado this incredible line, on which much of the filming for the Oscar-winning *Out of Africa* was carried out, plunges almost 4,000 feet in less than forty-two kilometres in a series of steep traverses down the contours of the Rift wall. With the complications of the First World War, it was not until 1 August 1915 that the line was handed over to the Uganda Railway — now Kenya Railways — which still operates it.

The saga of its construction is commemorated in an epic ballad by one of the rail gangs who, signing himself Korongo, tells something of the

Above: What the predators and other scavengers leave, the vultures — nature's undertakers — finish off.

spirit of those times and the sense of adventure, in the lyrical style of
Robert Service:

In the days to come, some remittance chum
May say to himself, 'I'll take
For a bit of fun just a railway run
And look at Magadi lake.'
When the snorting train shall awake the plain
And whistle and hiss and brake
How little he'll guess of the work and stress
That the railway took to make

Where the white rocks rang as we kept the gang
At work with pick and spade
Of the blasting fuse that we used to use,
The gelignite and the drill,
The culvert and bridge, the bank and ridge,
The cut in the marble hill . . .
Of the Saturday nights with gamble and fights
Of the lions we used to kill

I've said goodbye and I shall not try
To go back to those haunts again;
For I can recall ev'ry landscape small
As the lonely bush and plain,
As the wild beasts home, where the lions roam,
— Unquestioned their right to reign —
Now by day the smoke and by night the stroke
Of the piston declares the train.

Oh, I realize, that we civilize,
And the work we do is fine,
Then we lay the trails for the gleaming rails
Of a pioneering line.
But soon they'll push, till there's no more bush,
And never a bushman's shrine,
And when that day's come, where will be the home
For a soul that is made like mine . . .

Today the traveller makes his way down the smooth tarmac road —
built and maintained by the company which mines Magadi's soda
deposits — that climbs out of Nairobi around the southern shoulder of
the knuckle-shaped 8,000-foot-high Ngong Hills, which also featured
prominently in *Out of Africa*.

Rocky hills rise up out of the floor of the Valley, their lava soil covered
with stunted grass and thorn. From the air, Magadi's surface is like a
covering of crumpled, melted icing: mottled with patches of indigo red
where industrial excavators cut through the crust to haul up this
naturally recurring source of soda ash. Occasionally millions of flamingos
breed here, and the bleak but hauntingly beautiful landscapes around
have an astonishing wealth of bird life.

Left: Evaporated salt at Magadi, world's second largest source of trona after California's Salton Sea, swept into tidy lines to await collection for refining.

Below: With beautiful, lyrate horns, the impala is perhaps the most graceful of all antelopes.

Above: Baboons are extremely social and gregarious creatures, each troop led by a dominant male. In season the females mate indiscriminately, first with the junior males and then the more dominant seniors.

Its eastern shores are dominated by the little town the soda company has developed during the last eighty years — complete with posh residential suburbs, working-class flats, smart club with swimming pool, hospital, schools and a golf course with 'browns', a mixture of serried sludge and sump oil, instead of greens.

These soda lakes — Natron in Tanzania; Magadi, Elmenteita, and Turkana in Kenya — characterize this section of the Rift, which curves through the middle of the country from Turkana in the north to Magadi in the south, their surface heights varying in altitude from a few hundred feet to more than 6,000 feet above sea level.

The Maasai around Magadi, for instance, live several thousand feet lower than their kin seventy kilometres away at Naivasha, the highest and the purest of the Rift's Kenya lakes. The western buttress of the Rift at Magadi is formed by the formidable wall of the Nkuruman Escarpment topped by the Loita Hills.

No road climbs these rugged cliffs, yet the Maasai make their own trails up its almost sheer faces and through its thick forests to the top, where, beyond the Loita Hills, the land levels out in the Maasai Mara. Set more than 5,000 feet above sea level, these rolling grasslands form part of the Serengeti plains, which begin in the far south of Tanzania, and end at the foot of the Soit Ololol Escarpment at the north-western edge of the Mara.

These savannahs are recent features of the earth's flora. Today grasslands cover a quarter of the world — much of this in Africa and particularly in Kenya. They provide a perfect environment for the termites who labour wherever there are tropical grasslands. Their skin so sensitive to the sun they would shrivel in an instant, termites travel by tube — in tunnels they excavate beneath the savannah, carefully roofed with masticated mud. Termites are nature's architects. Their castles of clay — some rising higher than twenty feet — are intricate complexes of chambers, dining halls, and air-conditioning vents, which allow stale air

Above: Lower incisors of the hippopotamus, known as poor man's ivory. The teeth of this amphibious member of the pig family are formidable weapons.

Above: Hippo and young launch themselves into the Mara river. Stern disciplinarians, hippo mothers chastise their young with a savage bite.

to escape and recharge the dark passageways and cells with fresh air while maintaining humidity at the level which they need to survive. They achieve this by digging deep shafts — like wells in a castle compound — into the ground below, where workers collect the moisture.

How much these creatures celebrate water as a gift of life is vividly demonstrated during the first rains. They take wing and flutter in immense numbers in the night air — completely blacking out security lights on occasion. Some Kenyan folk regard them as a gourmet treat: many communities gather them up by the shovelful and fry them as tasty titbits.

The Mara's major feature is the annual 'migration' of more than a million wildebeest and attendant zebra, antelope, gazelle, and predators from the far south of Serengeti.

Nature's designers must have blown a fuse when they were creating these strange creatures. Given the front of an ox, the face of a jester, the beard of a mandarin, the rear of an antelope and the tail of the horse, both the wildebeest's appearance and its lunatic behaviour have earned it the title 'Clown of the Plains'. It's the star of the 'migration' — marching single-file in their hundreds of thousands, following the rains and the lush grasses northward until, between July and September, they arrive in the Mara.

There's no equal spectacle in animal Africa, and it's made the Mara the premier wildlife destination of the continent. Since the first lodge opened its doors at Keekorok in 1965, a rash of other lodges and tented camps have sprung up, threatening the delicate balance of the Mara's fragile grasslands and game species, especially that of the gentle cheetah.

The most specialized of the three killer cats, it's also the smallest — slender and more gentle in its demeanour. Cheetahs are easily domesticated, and for centuries were used in Arabia for hunting. Evolution has given the cheetah all the attributes it needs for speed —

89

Above: Ostrich and brood of young on the move through the Kenya grasslands. The largest living bird cannot fly, but it runs at up to sixty kilometres an hour. Often, however, they vanish abruptly from view — dropping suddenly into a squatting position and extending their necks along the ground.

Opposite top: Great white pelican wading with a gaggle of Egyptian geese.

Opposite left: Black-headed heron.

Opposite: Kori bustards, notable for ornamental plumes on head and neck.

deep chest, slender body and long, thin legs. Nothing in nature equals its swiftness on land.

The fastest animal in the world, the cheetah has recorded speeds of 112 kilometres an hour. But the burst is brief, always leaving it gasping for breath. Sometimes it is so short of breath, its victim escapes the capture hold — a slashing, claw-raking blow to the flank — and makes off. At other times, a more dominant killer or scavenger — lion or hyaena — will steal the kill from under its panting muzzle.

Now its peace disturbed, its land encroached, like the Maasai it's under pressure.

The Mara was once an essential part of the Maasai grazing lands, the people and their herds living in comfortable symbiosis with the wildlife. This latter-day advance of tourists has put increasing pressure on the traditional life styles of the Maasai, to whom the mountain at Namanga, ol Doinyo Orok, is sacred as the burial place of Mbatian, a one-eyed seer, or *laibon*, who in the nineteenth century unified the warring Maasai clans into a single society.

It was he, in a poetic but gloomy prophecy around the 1870s, who predicted the advent of the European and the plague of rinderpest and smallpox that decimated both the Maasai herds and the people. Mbatian warned of strangers of pink and the advance of a metal rhinoceros, together with malevolent diseases which combined would spell the end of Maasai society.

By the time the railway cut along the northern extremity of their territory in 1898, at Emali and Sultan Hamud, the rinderpest, first striking at the beginning of the decade, had virtually decimated the Maasai cattle. Smallpox cut their human numbers down to a handful of around 25,000 — and, like the Kamba, these proud people had to depend on hand-outs from the rail camps, and British administrators such as Ainsworth, for their survival. The Maasai never fully recovered from these disasters before their land was seized by the Europeans, and they

Left: Tawny eagle in Amboseli. Although a frequent scavenger at lion kills, the eagle also hunts for itself.

were moved on to their present territory only to be confronted with the demands of Independence.

Other ethnic groups in Kenya, like the Kamba, responded much more readily to the changes of the last century. The Kamba are ethnically related to the Kikuyu and speak a similar language. Their territory covers several thousand square kilometres of eastern Kenya, between Maasailand and the arid north-eastern deserts beyond Kitui, much of it drought prone.

Skilled wood-carvers, they produce many of the curios on sale in the shops and kiosks of Kenya's major towns. Hundreds of these craftsmen, *fundis*, work in a co-operative in Nairobi's Kamakunji area, turning out fine representations of wildlife and peoples in a matter of minutes: one man carving the body of an elephant, the other its trunk and ears, a third the legs. Some of their inlaid stools stand as works of art, lovingly worked and carved with stunning symmetry.

Latterly, the Kamba have usurped the martial traditions of the Maasai, serving with honour in the early colonial forces, during two World Wars and more recently providing a continuing cadre of officers and men for independent Kenya's Armed Forces, right up to the Chief of Staff.

It was Machakos, in the south-eastern lea of the beautiful Mua Hills, that Ainsworth fully expected Whitehouse to make his railhead — only to watch in astonishment as the platelayers took another direction and sped on to establish the railhead at the dismal fever-ridden swamp known to the Maasai as 'Nyrobi'.

If Whitehouse had done as Ainsworth, thirty-seven, anticipated, the history of Kenya would have been different and, some who live in Nairobi today would say, for the better.

4 · Shantytown Capital

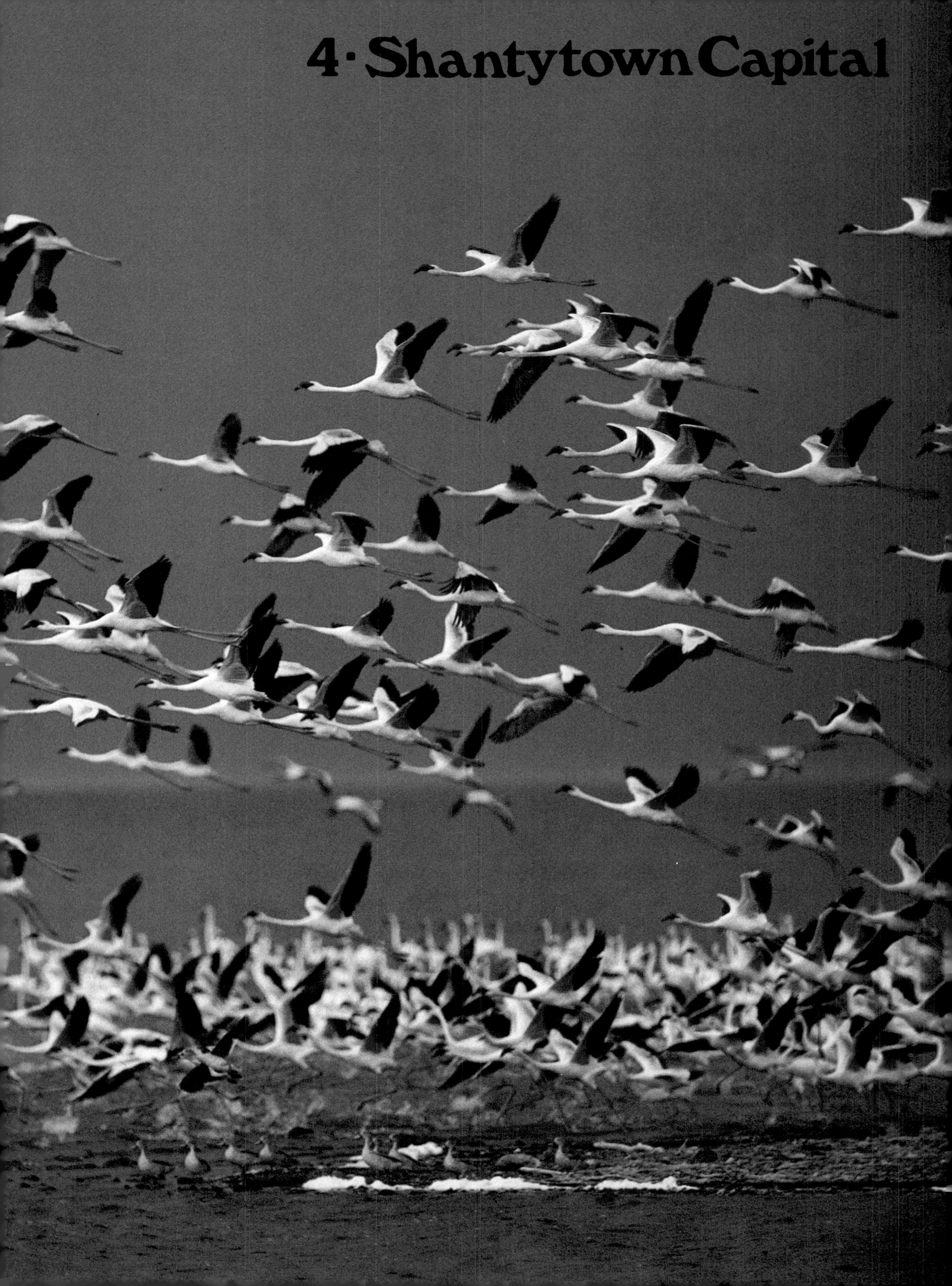

Opposite: *Dominated at left of picture by the 344-foot-high Kenyatta Conference Centre, Kenya's modern capital of Nairobi sprawls across the Kapiti Plains. Established as railhead in 1899, it was declared a township by Sir Arthur Hardinge, the British Vice-Consul in Zanzibar, in April 1901.*

It was 30 May 1899 when the 'Lunatic Line' reached the desolate swamp on the Athi Plains of East Africa, where the Maasai brought their herds to water. It was known to them as 'the place of cold waters'.

Machakos and Kikuyu, both pleasantly situated, surrounded by verdant and fertile hills, had been proposed as sites for the railhead, but Whitehouse ignored them. Blind to all but the immense requirements of manpower and material he would need to achieve one of the most remarkable engineering feats in the history of railway construction, he unerringly chose the most unhealthy spot within a radius of 150 kilometres. Nairobi's first permanent structure was a station, without a platform.

Around it, sprawling in the mud and filth that the work of construction created, a shantytown of tents and tin-and-timber huts sprang up. For its first decade, this now graceful capital with its broad malls, lined with palms and fringed with bougainvillea, spacious parks, gracious buildings and elegant suburbs, was a pestilent, disease-ridden slum, an ill-gotten child conceived from the seed of Imperial enterprise discharged into the fever-ridden wastes of Nairobi swamp.

To the men of the Uganda Railway, however, when the last rail was bolted down on its bed of sleepers on 30 May 1899 at 'the place of cold waters', only one thing mattered. This was railhead. A place in which to draw breath, to marshal all the many sinews of men and machines needed for the mighty enterprise ahead — a climb of 2,300 feet in forty-five kilometres to the forests that line the serrated cliffs overlooking the birthplace of mankind, the Rift Valley.

Until then, the only people at the swamp were the itinerant Maasai watering their herds, and Sergeant George Ellis, 39, from Newington Butts, Surrey, England, who ran the thatched stable that served as a transport depot for the Royal Engineers. The other residents were lions, mosquitoes, snakes, rodents, frogs and a handful of diseases, including the fatal blackwater fever.

Railhead was an empty place, the north-western fringe of a great alluvial plain. To the west it was bounded by the Ngong Hills. To the north-east, the Kamba's Mountain of the Buffalo, which is the Maasai's Ol Doinyo Sapuk, marked the other extremity of the Kaputei Plains; its forested dome reaching 7,000 feet into the sky.

Rivers leap from the western hills, draining down the valleys, through the forests, until they flash in the sunlight of the open savannah. These rills and streams used to rest in swamp before continuing the long journey east to the Indian Ocean. To the north beyond, the land rises sharply, once thick with forest, which was reached across a series of stepping stones set just above the swamp. It was a lonely post, but the soldier found it congenial enough. Ellis had been in Africa for many years, first in Nyasaland, where he had been a road builder. It was this skill which brought him to East Africa.

During his three years at Nyrobi — the spelling was changed to Nairobi by the Uganda Railways administration in October 1899 — he had entertained a surprising number of visitors, including the Reverend Fisher, who, in 1892 with Bishop Tucker, had found the remains of the murdered Bishop Hannington at Mumias. Fisher arrived at Ellis's camp in April 1898 with a small party from Uganda, including a missionary,

Below: *Nairobi's fast-growing Westlands suburb. The city centre lies beyond.*

Preceding pages: *Pink against the deep blue sky above Lake Bogoria, a flock of flamingos takes to the air in a vivid canvas of light, colour and movement.*

the Reverend E. Millar, a doctor and an army captain.

The year before that, Ellis played host to Dr Atkinson, who had travelled through Somalia with Lord Delamere and then left him at Baringo to come on alone to Ellis's post. During his stay in 1897, the doctor shot two lions in the Nairobi swamp and became enamoured of the area, particularly the first crest of hills just beyond the swamp, to which he returned within a year to establish a high-grade cattle breeding farm in Karura, the great forest where the elite suburb of Muthaiga now stands.

Just a month ahead of the railway, in April 1899, Delamere travelled up from the Athi River railhead — now an industrial town with abattoirs, distilleries, clothing factories — to observe that Nairobi was a splendid place for birds. He shot a great many before travelling on to Fort Smith, sixteen kilometres upcountry in the Kikuyu forest. This had been established in 1890 as a British outpost, heavily guarded.

The garrison, under Major Eric Smith, frequently rode down to Ellis's station in the company of Dr H. S. Boedeker, who had carved a farm out of the forest close to Fort Smith. There were others, too, in this strange assembly of African and European. Kitchin of the Smith Mackenzie trading company was busy experimenting with the company's new-born coffee plantation at Dagoretti — with stock taken from the nursery of the coffee plantation the White Fathers had set up in 1896 on land where the Loreto Convent now stands on St. Austin's Road. He was a black-bearded and mustachioed young man, clearly enjoying the challenge of Africa to the full.

There was Captain F. S. Dugmore, grey before his time in the African sun, who would ride down from his command at the palisaded Ngong Fort, and a burly Scotsman, Alex MacQueen, and his family, who had come across from their farm at Mbagathi — now part of Nairobi National Park. MacQueen sported a waist-length beard. He had vowed never to shave after trekking on to Uganda and losing everything. He and his wife had travelled to Nairobi some years earlier, most of the way on foot. There were others, perhaps remembered in some faded sepia picture of the time, whose purpose was unrecorded and whose presence has been forgotten.

There was Lenana, the Maasai's chief *laibon*, and there was Chief Waiyaki, head of the Dagoretti Kikuyu clans, who had his enclave at Kinoo on the hill overlooking Fort Smith. There are contemporary pictures, in albums and collections and little-known publications, of many such people. In one photograph there are C. R. W. Lane and Mrs James Martin, sultry, attractive but thick-browed wife of the illiterate Maltese sailmaker who first crossed these parts sixteen years before in the company of James Thomson. (In time he became one of the hardy breed of Britain's first District Commissioners.) There is also Lieutenant F. G. Hall, who founded Fort Hall — now Murang'a — and a Goan, D'Silva, ferret-faced, cloth-capped. He became Nairobi's greatest philanthropist, universally known as Baba Dogo, and universally mourned after his death in the late 1970s. In the same picture, seated on the ground, is an arrogant, elegantly mustachioed man with intelligent, piercing eyes but without name.

98　　These African warriors, herdsman and farmers, these European

Above: Fiery apostle of man's beginnings, Dr Louis Leakey. His statue stands outside the National Museum in Nairobi.

Above: Nairobi's streets awash in a blaze of jacaranda blossoms, legacy of a short-serving city administrator of the 1920s remembered only as 'Jacaranda Jim'.

loners, these itinerant Goans and Asians, these missionaries and military men, formed a motley and bizarre group. But they had one thing in common. They were the first citizens of Nairobi.

It was thick with lion, leopard, cheetah, buffalo, rhinoceros, zebra and a multitude of other animals. Seven of the victims in the little cemetery started by the railhead workers were taken by lion, an eighth by rhinoceros.

In these early years, a roaring lion once treed a security guard, *askari*, up a lamppost outside the railway headquarters. One of Nairobi's first policemen, Robert Foran, returning at midnight from dinner at the Nairobi Club on 'The Hill', surveyed the scene, knocked on his disbelieving neighbour's door, borrowed a rifle and, clad in patent leather shoes, dinner suit and bow tie, despatched the beast — to the eternal thanks of the hapless African guard. On another occasion, a lioness and cubs took refuge under the General Post Office, a wooden building raised on stilts, and Foran again came to the rescue, killing the lioness and adopting the surviving cub as a pet.

No doubt its scions live on in Nairobi National Park, 110 square kilometres of pristine, virgin wilderness almost wholly within the metropolitan area. Bordered on the western side by the suburbs of Karen and Langata, in the north by Wilson Airport and the city itself, and on its eastern side by the Mombasa Road and the factories of industrial giants like Firestone and General Motors, lion still stalk the park's savannah and forest. It's one of the great experiences of a Kenya safari to come upon a pride feasting on a kill not more than four kilometres from the

Opposite: Dove of peace at centre of Kenya's Uhuru monument in Uhuru Gardens, Nairobi, built to commemorate the nation's first twenty years of freedom.

crowded city centre high-rise offices and pavements thronging with shoppers.

Despite its shantytown origins, Nairobi is indeed a memorable capital — both in its setting and the contrasts and experiences it affords. Five hundred kilometres from the coast, Nairobi is around 5,500 feet above sea level. Its metropolitan area covers 689 square kilometres, from the Embakasi plains in the east and up the once wooded slopes of the eastern wall of the Great Rift Valley in the west. Jomo Kenyatta International Airport, one of the busiest in Africa, lies to the east in the lea of the Lukenia Hills and Ol Doinyo Sapuk, and the glide path brings the giant jetliners low over the national park.

As it began so it remains, a vibrant cosmopolitan mixture of cultures and customs pleasantly warmed by the Equatorial sun and growing at a phenomenal rate. When it was raised to city status on the occasion of its Golden Jubilee on 30 March 1950, with letters patent presented by the Duke of Gloucester, the population was under 500,000. Thirty years later, according to the most recent census, it had more than doubled, and it was anticipated that by the end of the century it would reach between four and five million.

The attractively laid-out three-square-kilometre city centre is dominated by the twenty-nine-storey, 344-foot-high outline of the Kenyatta International Conference Centre, which draws its inspiration from both rural Africa and ancient Rome: the interior is laid out with indoor fountain pools and red-tiled promenades. At one side of the hexagonal tower is a superbly appointed amphitheatre shaped like an African hut, *rondavel*, and the main plenary hall, a modern version of the Senate, can seat 4,000 delegates. From the revolving restaurant-bar at the top of the tower, every perspective of this city in the sun slowly passes by in a 360° panorama.

At the eastern edge of the city centre are the classical neo-colonial lines of the 1929 Kenya Railways Headquarters and the station where it all began. Along Moi Avenue, a curious mixture of early buildings, still roofed with corrugated iron, are juxtaposed among the modern office blocks and hotels. In 1987, at the western end, close to the university, some of the tin huts from which John Ainsworth, Nairobi's first administrator, shaped the outline of the city, still stood. His legacy survives in the eucalyptus and jacaranda that line the streets and in the small park opposite the huts. Jeevanjee Gardens became the city's first recreational space, donated by the public benefactor and philanthropist, A. M. Jeevanjee, who made his fortune as a railway contractor, after the bazaars that stood there were consumed in a tinder-brush fire.

In March 1906, the Duke of Connaught unveiled a statue of his mother, Queen Victoria, which now watches over lunchtime crowds, draped on bench or lawn, listening to the impromptu sermons of itinerant preachers with loud-hailers. The park is close to the city's fruit and vegetable market and its first bazaar area.

More shops, cinemas, clubs and hotels line the city's main thoroughfare. Kenyatta Avenue began as Sixth Avenue, was renamed Delamere Avenue after the fiery settler who pioneered the country's farming, and finally after Mzee Jomo Kenyatta, founding father of free Kenya.

Above: Statue of Kenya's founding father, Mzee Jomo Kenyatta, dominates the forecourt of the Kenyatta International Conference Centre.

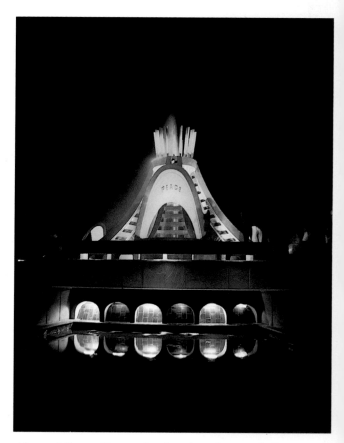

Above: Uhuru Fountain, bearing the words Peace, Love and Unity, in the grounds of Nairobi's Uhuru Park opposite Parliament Buildings.

*Below: Colourful pageant as team forms the map of
Kenya at the opening of the 1987 All-Africa Games at
Moi International Sports Complex, Kasarani,
Nairobi.*

On the other side of the city centre is Haile Selassie Avenue, formerly Sergeant Ellis Avenue, which crosses Uhuru Highway, part of the planned trans-African highway from Mombasa to Lagos, and climbs 'The Hill' past the Railway Club, Kenya's first Parliament. It was here in 1899 that the first game of cricket was played in Nairobi. Up the hill, there's another survivor of the old city, Nairobi Club. Not far from its 1913 club house is the city's oldest golf course. The Royal Nairobi Golf Club, laid out in 1906, was given its royal accolade by Edward VIII in 1936.

The whole of this hill area, dry and forested, was claimed by Whitehouse when the Railway arrived in Nairobi. Hearing of this, Ainsworth rode up from Machakos and removed the peg stakes which had been hammered in on the instructions of Whitehouse as he and Whitehouse shouted at each other. Whitehouse claimed it was Railway land, Ainsworth that it was sovereign land: both forgetting it was African land. Announcing his intention to protect the Crown interests, Ainsworth at once set up his administrative headquarters in Nairobi.

The city's present shape grew out of a 1948 master plan, endowing it with a permanent ribbon of green along the western side of Uhuru Highway. This included the nine-hole Railway Golf Club course laid out in 1920, an international sports stadium, one of the major venues for the 1987 All Africa Games, two parks, the university playing fields and the last remnants of the once fecund Chiromo Forest. With new campus buildings and private estates under construction, there's not much of it left now, the last giant blue gums felled by the axe.

But it's worth the ride to City Park, a remnant forest which sported leopard as recently as 1980 and was excised by John Ainsworth as public land as early as 1904 to provide, well within the heart of the city, a sylvan retreat where vervet monkeys gambol among the picnickers.

It's near here that the National Museum — on top of a small hill overlooking one of the city's oldest hotels, the Norfolk, opened on Christmas Day 1904 — mounts its impressive exhibitions: including one on the origins of mankind traced back to the distant shores of Lake Turkana. Alongside the Museum is a snake park stocked with poisonous and non-poisonous reptiles, including deadly mambas, cobras, and puff adders.

Near Nairobi Station there's another museum — dedicated to the story of the Lunatic Express — with exhibitions that include the bric-a-brac of the race to Lake Victoria, old steam locomotives, the cow-catcher on which Winston Churchill, Teddy Roosevelt and later the Prince of Wales rode in style, and the coach from which young Inspector Charles Ryall was dragged to his death.

To the west, directly beneath the Conference Centre, are Kenya's Parliament Buildings where the country's 188 elected and twelve nominated MPs meet to debate the crucial issues affecting this young nation. On the north side of the Conference Centre is the City Hall, where the Duke of Gloucester presented the charter elevating Nairobi to a city. Built in 1938, it was badly damaged by fire in 1985.

The north-east side of this city centre, Victoria Street, renamed Tom Mboya Street in memory of the slain Kenya political leader, marks the dividing line between smart downtown capital and the origins of the first bazaar and shanty in Nairobi, which spread down to the Nairobi River.

103

It's here that the capital's African ambience comes to vivid life. Open-fronted shops display colourful wares and cupboard-size radio shops blare out the latest Swahili music hits night and day. Some eating houses, serving ethnic stews of *sukuma wiki* (spinach) and beef — and *matumbo* (tripe) — also operate around the clock. One even has no doors, removed because the proprietor saw no sense in them since the premises never closed.

Not far away is the colourful market area of Kamakunji, close to the city's country bus station. In one corner, hundreds of artisans convert scrap metal into *sufurias* — saucepans — and old tyres into sandals, favoured by the shoeless Maasai. The warriors name them for the distance they endure before wearing out, thus favourites are known as Loitokitok, far away on the slopes of Kilimanjaro, or perhaps as Kajiado, the southern administrative capital of Maasailand.

It's a carnival of honky-tonk noise — blaring radios, record-players, loud-hailers, the raucous cries of the sidewalk vendors and the *manamabas*, call boys, luring passengers to the country buses and the ubiquitous freelance *matatus*, Kenya's version of the West African 'mammy wagons' which supplement the inadequate public transport systems. A riot of garish colour, painted with the vivid hues of cheap plastic and cloth items, floods the sidewalks and stalls with brilliant splashes.

It's not far from the spot where Nairobi's first race meeting was held — when even pack horses were enlisted to enliven the event and make up a decent field — in 1901. It became a twice-yearly gymkhana meeting, but several times starts were delayed by wild game on the track — rhinoceros, lion and others. The course at Kariokor — so named after the Carrier Corps, which served during the First World War — did service for half a century, until the Jockey Club of Kenya acquired the Ngong

Above: Nairobi's Anglican All Saints Cathedral took many years to build on funds raised voluntarily.

Racecourse in the west of the city, said by many to be the most beautiful race track in the Commonwealth. There are now meetings forty-four Sundays a year, and the bloodstock has been refined over the years by imported thoroughbreds.

Dinghies sail regularly on the dark waters of Nairobi Dam, hastily built just after the Second World War to boost the municipal water supplies, but no longer used as such. Outlined against the graceful sails of the vessels is the Kibera shantytown on the north bank of the dam. The colonial authorities presented this land in 1922 to the city's Nubian population — to mark appreciation for their service and loyalty in the 1914-18 war. Now it's home for hundreds of thousands of urban poor.

At Ruaraka, on the north-east perimeter of the city, Chinese and Kenyan workers put the finishing touches to an Olympic Stadium of impressive proportions just before the 1 August 1987 start of the All Africa Games. Eventually, this national sports complex — which will include facilities for not only soccer and athletics but a host of other sports — will be the finest in Africa.

Thirty minutes out of town to the west, the visitor can walk along the ridge of the Ngong Hills, gazing down the western slopes which drop thousands of feet to the floor of the Great Rift Valley. Maasai legend says that this range of folded hills, shaped like the knuckles of a clenched fist, were formed when a giant tripped over Kilimanjaro, more than 250 kilometres south-east, and clawed at the earth when he fell.

Once lushly forested, these have been taken for smallholdings, and only remnant copses of the Hills' ancient trees dot the top. But there are stunning views of the drop into the Rift, which here descends abruptly to little more than a thousand feet above sea level.

It was on the eastern slopes of these hills that Karen Blixen settled with her husband, Baron Bror Blixen, in 1913 to establish a coffee farm, which she abandoned — penniless — in the 1930s. Her experiences, and her love affair with Denys Finch Hatton, inspired the book *Out of Africa*, which she wrote as Isak Dinesen. The suburb covering her old coffee farm bears her name, Karen. The house she left is now a museum in her honour, restored to the style in which she maintained it. And the monument she built to the memory of Finch Hatton — a simple obelisk — still stands, marking his grave on her beloved Ngong Hills, now amid the maize stalks of one of the smallholders who have since settled this area.

North-east of Karen are Kabete and Fort Smith, the stockaded fort built by the British in 1890. It stands on a winding tarmac trail which was once the dirt lane named Sclater's Road, after the English officer and his men — including Sergeant Ellis — who blazed a trade route up the shoulders of the Rift wall, through the thick, impenetrable forest of the Kikuyu.

Naturally, the Kikuyu were hostile to this invasion and, across the road from the fort, a maize field contains the neglected marble graves of three Britons, one of them killed by the Kikuyu who used to besiege the fort. It's mellowed now, used as a private residence, and the fig tree planted by the Kikuyu chief Kinyanjui with the British officer as a symbol of peace casts a peaceful shade over the former fortress — symbol of the friendship which endures after Kenya's Independence.

Now the forests on these slopes have gone, transformed into Kiambu 105

and Tigoni's lush, meadow-like farmlands, where Kenya's first full-scale tea and coffee plantations were established just after the turn of the century. This precious land sold at about ten acres a Kenya shilling when the first European settlers arrived. All this fertile and scenic landscape was bounteous, and it was at Githunguri and Gatundu, in Kiambu District, that Kenya's founding father Mzee Jomo Kenyatta made his home. One of the Kiambu ridges is famous for the quality of Kenya's already renowned coffee. The berries grown here are regarded as the *crème de la crème* of all the world's coffees and, whatever the fluctuations in world prices, command the highest prices of all. Not for nothing is this ridge, between Banana Hill and Tigoni, known as Millionaires' Row.

Altitude and rainfall are the regulating factors in the quality of coffee. Kenya coffee is regarded as the world's finest and is used to beef up the bouquet and flavour of the robustas from which the major coffee blends are made. The higher uplands of Limuru from Tigoni are ideal for tea. Other major coffee regions are Murang'a and Nyeri districts. These districts are also known for tea, although the bulk of this crop is grown in the Kericho and Nandi Hills. These two crops are Kenya's major foreign currency earners.

The railway survey parties basically followed the alignment of Sclater's Road, passing close to Fort Smith — the line has since been realigned and now cuts through Dagoretti and Kikuyu — on the 2,000-foot climb through Tigoni and Limuru to the crest of the Rift Escarpment in less than forty kilometres.

As the track inched out of the shantytown capital-to-be in the middle

Above: Interior of the Hindu Jain Temple in the Nairobi suburb of Ngara.

Opposite: Jamia Mosque in the heart of downtown Nairobi.

of 1899, it was a formidable task to ascend such a height in that short distance. But even this feat of engineering paled beside the awesome challenge awaiting the engineers when they reached the top. In many places the escarpment plunges almost sheer, between 1,000 and 3,000 feet, to the valley floor.

Engineer Ronald Preston — whose wife Florence braved the perils of the wild to keep him company throughout the five-and-a-half years it took to build the line — devised an ingenious ramp and pulley system which lowered supply trains and line workers, enabling the railhead to move on ahead up the Rift Valley while the permanent line was laid on a more gentle descent. At a critical time when the line was way behind schedule, it saved months of delay.

The dramatic story of this railway — unsurpassed for drama and adventure — is told in several books: Ronald Hardy's *The Iron Snake*, Charles Miller's *The Lunatic Express* and, for railway buffs, by Alastair Matheson in Mohamed Amin and Duncan Willetts's picture book, *Railway Across the Equator*.

It's from the top of this escarpment that the Rift unfolds in all its rugged grandeur, the hazy blue-grey of the Mau Escarpment, fifty kilometres away on the western wall of this great chasm in the world's surface, rising up amid an armada of clouds, galleons of the sky sailing by in graceful haste.

In the foreground, the space-age antennae of Kenya's satellite earth station stand against the backdrop of the dormant volcanoes of Susua and Longonot, two of a chain of volcanoes — a necklace of molten

108

Above: Alert cheetah family in Nairobi National Park.

Opposite: The zebra's eye-catching stripes are unique among nature's handiwork. Among the many millions which roam Africa, no two are alike.

Overleaf: Knife-edged rim of 9,109-foot-high Longonot, a dormant volcano in the Great Rift Valley. Raging steam beds beneath its ravaged flanks have been tapped in Africa's largest geothermal project and now supply a substantial portion of the national power requirements.

magma and restless fire simmering not far beneath the valley's crust —
that stretches the length of the Kenya Rift, extending from Tanzania in
the south to Ethiopia in the north.

While Preston took a direct route down the escarpment, the
permanent way followed the alignment of the wall in a gradual descent,
establishing one railhead about three-quarters of the way down, at a
place called Kijabe. Not long after this, missionaries of an evangelistic
American sect established the first of the African Inland Mission bases,
under strict rules of abstinence but not celibacy. Polygamy was — and in
many instances still is — a traditional way of life. The missions have
always been careful first to catch their converts before reforming their
traditional ways.

Where Theodore Roosevelt laid the mission foundation stone in 1909
— after an exhilarating ride on the cowcatcher of his train — this sleepy
monastic community is ruled by a council of elders who still invoke the
same ordinances. There's a model community hospital — funded by
mission money and overseas donations — but no shop sells tobacco or
liquor. Kijabe is as dry as the Mormon's Salt Lake City in America but, in
Kijabe, polygamy is no longer sanctified.

Though it's no more than sixty kilometres from the capital, in the
perspective of time and environment it could be another world. When
drought struck Kenya in 1984, citizens were kept indoors — or walked at
their peril. Rampaging forest buffaloes herded down into the town in
search of grazing and water. The hospital was kept busy with casualties
who had been gored.

The almost sheer forested wall of the Rift rises up behind Kijabe, but in
the opposite direction there are splendid views of the twin volcanoes.

Lying close to one another, Longonot and Susua were the models for
the Sheba's Breasts mountains in *King Solomon's Mines*. Like the book's
warriors, Alan Quartermain filched the setting from Joseph Thomson's
enthralling *Walk through Maasailand*, the account of his epic expedition
from Mombasa to Baringo, Mount Elgon, western Kenya and back to
Mombasa.

Kenya's earth satellite station stands to the south-east of Longonot,
which Thomson climbed during his 1883 trek north. The views from its
knife-edge rim are spectacular. He was overcome with vertigo and
experienced an irresistible urge to throw himself down into the abyss.
The name comes from the Maasai, *oloonong'ot*, meaning mountain of
many spurs. Longonot's rumpled flanks are creased with dozens of
ridges and studded with parasitic cones. The climb to the top and around
the rim is a stiff four to five hours walking. At 9,000 feet, the air is already
beginning to thin out and lungs labour.

There's an inner 'lost world' in the crater. A pilot who flew beneath the
level of the rim, to circle inside, dared too much. Caught in the
downdrafts that hurtle over its rim, he never emerged. Similar brave
spirits swing across the chasm of Susua to reach its inner plateau — a
dead ringer for Conan Doyle's Pleistocene relic of the age of dinosaurs.

The floor of Longonot is an unviolated wildlife retreat, and you can
scramble down the almost sheer crater wall in about ten minutes. But few
hazard the descent through the scrub forest and thorn at the bottom
where wild buffalo are thick on the ground.

*Above: Satellite ground station in Rift Valley at a
height of more than 6,000 feet above sea level. Kenya's
space communication system was among the first in
Africa.*

Above: Eccentric legacy of a zany colonial past, Ginger Bell's Hounds in Nairobi's forested suburbs — the hunted is no fox but a fast-running servant dragging a lure of aniseed bags.

Until recently, the crater floor and the slopes outside were notable for their frequent steam vents. Fiery Longonot is only sleeping and the nascent energy beneath its rumbling crown has now been tapped in Africa's only geothermal project. Ground waters, several thousand feet beneath the surface, record an astonishing 304°C — one of the hottest temperatures recorded. You can check these out on the southern slopes, where fingers of steam from the boreholes rise into the sky in staccato jets.

The landscape around Longonot's slopes, though close to large population centres, is as wild as any in Kenya. Hell's Gate, a dramatic gorge with sheer red cliffs and a grassy floor where buffalo, hartebeest, gazelle, zebra and eland still graze and browse, is dominated by the volcanic plug of Fischer's Tower, named after the German who explored this region in the 19th century. It's a stunning rock climb fraught with peril. There's another similar obelisk, Ol Basta, which was exposed when the lava around it eroded, and from there the gorge is just a tangled, near-impassable ravine.

If you come across fibreglass boulders and rocks among the genuine articles don't be too surprised. A film crew chose Hell's Gate in the early 1980s as one of the locations for *Sheena — Queen of the Jungle* and, in typical Hollywood fashion, decided that nature's handiwork needed an assist from their props department.

The railway line passes the eastern base of Longonot, but thousands of feet above rides a new scenic highway that crests the escarpment at almost 9,000 feet. Dark clouds often boil and billow over the rim of Longonot during the rainy season, grasping it with icy fingers before rolling on across the gulf and over the facing escarpment, which is almost at the same height.

Beyond, spread out over 110 square kilometres, a pearl in the bosom of the Kenya Rift, the waters of Lake Naivasha glisten silver as the sun slopes swiftly towards the west. Purest and highest of all the Rift lakes, Naivasha is a popular water resort and bird sanctuary without peer. Over 400 species have been recorded here: more than the entire list of birds seen in the British Isles.

You can take a cabin cruiser, outboard dinghy, or sailboat and enjoy cruising at an altitude of more than 6,000 feet without leaving the surface; drop anchor off one of the papyrus islands that float on the lake's surface and fish for sporting black bass or tilapia. Look around — there's a good chance you'll see a curious, long-legged bird walking across the water. It will be an African jacana, known as a lily-trotter, a marvellous example of the versatility of nature and evolution. Its widespread feet, with very extended toes, enable it to walk on water-lily leaves and other lacustrine vegetation.

Great white pelicans lumber across the water, leaden giants straining to escape gravity in ponderous flight, wings beating frantically to avoid a shame-faced stall. With mincing gait, herons stalk the diminutae at the shore's edge. Cormorants and ducks bob on the ruffled surface while a fish eagle screeches and, with an ecstatic swoop dives downward to snatch, from just beneath the water's surface, a tilapia in its talons. Then, full throttle, it climbs powerfully without pause, banking in an exuberant display of gymnastic flight, to alight unflurried on its perch.

It was on these shores that Joy Adamson fostered Elsa and her cubs, the heroine of her wildlife classic, *Born Free*. Now her home, Elsamere, is a living memorial — a wildlife education centre and museum to the woman brutally murdered at Shaba National Reserve in Kenya's north in 1980.

It's not far from a rambling country home framed by yellow fever trees in thirteen hectares of gardens, shrubs, flowers and verdant lawns which sprawl down to the lake. Just after the war, this was Kenya's international air terminal when the great Short flying boats of British Overseas Airways flew leisurely along the course of the Nile and on down to South Africa. They landed at Naivasha, where passengers were ferried ashore before the eighty-four kilometre road journey to Nairobi. Now it's a five-star safari hotel.

Apart from tourism, Lake Naivasha is fount of one of Kenya's great agro-industries. It's here that Kenya's fledgling wine industry has taken root. Carefully tended vineyards established since 1980 produce vintage Naivasha wines. Its waters irrigate thousands of hectares of fertile volcanic loam which burgeon with vegetables and colourful flowers. During the high season, more than a million stems a night are airlifted to winterbound Europe, tokens of the tropical sun that warm thousands of icebound homes with their colour and fragrance.

Above its western shores, rising 9,365 feet above sea level, the brooding bulk of Opuru marks the great massif of the Mau Escarpment. Settlement and development are taking their toll on the primal forests which clothed these heights. The climb is steep, the road precipitous.

Above: Marked by boiling geysers on its western shores and sheer 2,000-foot-high cliffs on its eastern shores, coloured pink by flocks of flamingos, Lake Bogoria remains unspoilt.

116

Where once ancient podocarpus and cedar spread their roots on the rich forest floor, their gnarled limbs roped with lianas and other parasitic growth, wheat and barley stretch as far as the eye can see. Above the wheat fields, more forest has been cleared for potatoes. The damp chill mists and rich soil nourish their growth.

Large tracts of forest still remain, foot trails winding below the cathedral-like arches of the tall branches, motes of sun streaming through and, here and there, occasional glades cleared by peasant farmers for their thatched homesteads and subsistence smallholdings.

For thousands of years these forests have been the home of a small group of hunter-gatherers, the Okiek, known to the Maasai by the contemptuous name of *il Torrobo*, which has been corrupted into Dorobo. They claim ancestral ownership of much of the Mau forest. They hunt with bows, using poisonous arrows, and traps, living off wild fruit, plants and wild honey. To capture the elephant that once occupied the Mau, they dug deep pits and lined the bottom with poisoned spears. They also practise pottery in their temporary huts — a dome made of a framework of sticks covered with animal skins.

At the escarpment's edge, the forest stops and the walls plunge down. Southward, the Mau slopes down to Narok, gateway to Maasai Mara and district headquarters of this area of Maasailand. All the land around here is Kenya's granary — endless fields of wheat and barley stretch as far as the eye can see. The advance of the twentieth century was largely ignored by the Maasai until recently, but Narok's growth in the last decade — banks, schools, tarmac roads — is evidence of their swift embrace of the modern world and its benefits.

Preston took his track east of Naivasha, in the western lea of one of Kenya's greatest mountain massifs, Nyandarua, its highest point reaching more than 13,000 feet above sea level. These mountain moorlands, dominated by a forty-six-kilometre-long plateau between its two highest points, so reminded Joseph Thomson of his Scottish heath that he named them the Aberdares — after the President of the Royal Geographical Society, who had sent him to investigate the fables of snow on the Equator which so outraged Britain's Victorian scientists and geographers.

It was from Naivasha, seventeen years before Preston, in the glow of a false dawn, a few minutes before the sun exploded into light behind the mountain and began its swift climb to its zenith, that Thomson trudged up through the frost that rimmed the giant heather tussock, wary of the belligerent buffalo and elephant that still roam these heights, to marvel at the glittering scene which greeted him as he reached the top of the Aberdares. Early morning light on the Equator has a startling clarity.

Everything in Kenya seems to have been created as a natural spectacle without its like anywhere. The ordered, metronome regularity — twelve hours of day, twelve of night — of life at the Equator seems to have been ordained as the perfect rhythm of wakefulness and sleep.

Thus did Thomson get his first glimpse of Africa's second highest point, Mount Kenya, its twin spires of Batian and Nelion thrusting into the sky directly above the Equator, wearing a glistening necklace of ice that stretched gracefully around them, with the Lewis Glacier like a jewel at its throat. Batian, separated by a knife-edge ridge and a few feet from

17,022-foot-high Nelion, touches 17,058 feet.

Three decades later, another line, thrusting north out of Nairobi, would cross the Equator and embed itself high on the shoulders of this magical mountain, but in 1900, Preston's eyes were fixed firmly on the west, as the track headed out of Naivasha to Gilgil where Thomson had taken the high pass through the Aberdares north to Baringo.

As a town, Gilgil's two claims to fame are its country club and the Commonwealth War Cemetery, where about 200 victims of the Second World War are buried — one of forty such cemeteries in Kenya maintained immaculately by the Commonwealth War Graves Commission.

When he was at Gilgil, however, Preston was not contemplating the beauty of the remarkable wild and untouched countryside around him, but the massive challenge of grafting a railway line onto the wall and floor of the Rift Valley. Out of Gilgil, the track clung to the side of the Rift scarp. Though they never realized it, the coolies digging the foundations were cutting up ground significant to the history of mankind.

On the lip of the scarp just beyond Gilgil, in the strata of the cliff face and on the valley floor, are many prehistoric sites, including Kariandusi, with a number of *in situ* Acheulian tool exhibits, which was cleared by Louis Leakey in 1928. There's also a mine which excavates diatomite, a startlingly white chalk-like rock composed of billions of compressed silica, the skeletons of the microcospic sea organisms — diatoms — which flourished here hundreds of millions of years ago and now serve as filters for water and brewing industries and as a non-toxic insecticide in grain stores.

The mine offices overlook the shallow soda lake of Elmenteita, which dries up completely during long droughts. It often seems to be a shimmering sea of pink, its alkaline waters luring hundreds of thousands of flamingos.

One of the old slave caravan routes from Lake Victoria to the Coast ran through this part of the Rift along the shores of Elmenteita and features vividly in Rider Haggard's *King Solomon's Mines*. It's easy to imagine this kind of adventure yarn as a reality when you explore the catacombs carved into the cliff by the mining operations, which began in the 1940s. Walk down these shafts, which glint eerily white, as hundreds of bats flutter about, and just for a moment you can believe that a horde of Maasai are gathered outside — angry at the white interloper.

The views from the mine headquarters are spectacular. In Preston's time, the land seemed endless, and eventually all this area, including Elmenteita, formed the vast Soysambu estate of Lord Delamere, the Cheshire-born peer who sank his wealth and his life into pioneering Kenya's farm industry: a legacy which flourishes today in the hands of its indigenous owners. Few African states are as productive or bountiful as Kenya's central highlands.

Whatever Delamere's early twentieth-century views of Kenya's future destiny — his biography by Elspeth Huxley is called *White Man's Country* — his passion for this land was all-consuming. He sank his boundless energy into one agricultural project after another. The giant milling conglomerate, Unga, which now provides the bulk of the nation's maize
118 flour, wheat and bread, was established because of his vision and

Above: Okiek hunter in the forests of the Mau Escarpment which forms the eastern wall of the Rift Valley.

enterprise. Delamere was not alone in his infatuation and lifelong love of Kenya. It was the flesh and blood of all — Maasai, Kalenjin, Kikuyu, Nandi, Kipsigis, Gusii, Meru, Kamba — who lived within its previously undrawn boundaries.

Three years after Preston's platelayers passed Elmenteita, Delamere rode out to stake his first claim to 4,047 hectares of prime land, 'Equator Ranch', some distance beyond Elmenteita around Njoro, thus setting in motion the events that would culminate in the most determined freedom struggle in African history.

By then the Uganda Railway had been in existence for more than two years. Soon after Elmenteita, Preston and his coolies arrived on a bleak and open plain known to the Maasai as *Enakuro*, 'the place of the swirling dust'. Today Nakuru is Kenya's fourth largest town, perched on the slopes of the Menengai Crater, the second largest volcanic caldera in the world, overlooking the seasonal Lake Nakuru, which varies in size from five to thirty square kilometres depending on the rains.

It was during one of Kenya's cyclical wet spells that ornithologist and artist Peter Scott arrived on these fluctuating shores to marvel at a sight he described as the greatest bird spectacle in the world. There, wading in the shallows, floating a little way offshore, with more still circling on the Rift thermals, was a cloud of amorphous blush pink — a million or more flamingos.

This forty-square-kilometre haven, declared a national park, flourished as a result of Scott's acclaim, and still does — though when the dry seasons set in the flamingos vanish. It's only when the levels of water and the algae on which they feed are balanced that they assemble in such masses.

But they are never too far away for those prepared to look. If Elmenteita's level is right the birds will be there; if not, they'll be over the hills and floating on Lake Bogoria in the Rift or in the shallow soda pan of Lake Logipi in Suguta Valley, just south of Lake Turkana. If none of these, then perhaps at Lake Magadi, or Tanzania's Lake Natron.

Not just bird life flourishes in Nakuru. The wooded cliffs and shores surrounding it host rhinoceros, leopard, lion, giraffe and hippo. The woods give Nakuru its character, and here you may be lucky enough to come across the largest of African snakes — the python — which kills, like the boa, by squeezing its victims to death.

The slopes of Menengai host another prehistoric museum, Hyrax Hill, which has *in situ* exhibits from many ages, including the Neolithic and Iron. Above this fascinating display of most of the ages of man, uncovered where they were left, you'll arrive at the dramatic rim of the Menengai, plunging down to the bush floor within a thousand feet or more and stretching across from wall to wall more than twelve kilometres. One of the great Maasai clan battles of the nineteenth century — the Ilpurko versus the Ilaikipiak — was fought here, and the soughing of the wind over the crater rim is said to be the sad and haunted cries of those slain in battle.

But when Preston arrived at Nakuru there was no settlement of any kind. Photographs show a desolate empty plain that begins abruptly at the end of the first platform that was built 'as if,' writes Alastair Matheson in *Railway across the Equator*, 'the bare and mysterious land

beyond was forbidden territory'.

It was not until the early 1920s that a new line began to snake out of Nakuru directly to the Uganda border to tap this rich source of railway freight. From this, in 1926 an improbable branch line swept down from Rongai on the northern facing slopes of Menengai Crater to the Rift Valley floor. The wayside halts along the way — Kampi ya Moto, McCall's Sidings, Ol Punyata, Milton's Sidings — created the impression that this was in fact the personal fiefdom of the local settlers.

It came to rest at Solai with something of a bang, for in 1928 an earthquake struck the Rift with such force that, at Solai, it created a bottomless void in the earth's surface — fortunately only thirty centimetres across.

From Rongai, the main track climbs the eastern face of the western Rift wall in a series of twisting, tortuous loops through the cool, dark sanctuaries of the Timboroa forests, reaching the highest point of any railway in the Commonwealth, 9,135 feet, before crossing the Equator at 8,716 feet on the high, level plateau of the Uasin Gishu and the Trans-Nzoia.

Prosperous farm communities exist in this highland wonderland, with names that snap off the tongue — Kapkut, Kapsabet, and Kaptagat — reflecting the Elgeyo's tenancy by the Kalenjin group of peoples. Kapkut lies close to Eldama Ravine, where Thomson's lieutenant, James Martin, took up office as the first British District Officer long before the railway passed that way.

120   Just a few kilometres east of the track as it heads on to Eldoret lies one

Above: One of two freshwater lakes in the Kenya Rift, the muddy waters of Lake Baringo are fished by the Njemps, a breakaway group of Maasai pastoralists who abandoned their nomadic life to become fishermen.

Above: Adept camouflage artist — the striking
Chamaeleo dilepis.

of the most dramatic scarps in the world — the Elgeyo Escarpment of the Rift stretches more than 120 kilometres — which in places drops sheer more than 8,000 feet to the valley floor.

North of Kapkut — little distant from the railway line — great bluffs rise up at either side on a precipitous cliff known as World's End. The name is apt. The heat dances in the shimmering air as the wind tugs viciously at your shirt sleeves. Martial birds and raptors circle on the constant thermals that blast up the face of the cliff and across the plateau.

Before you is a void that stuns the senses and clutches at the stomach; awesome and inspiring. Far below, thousands of feet beneath the edge of this dizzying drop, unfolds the infinite sweep of the tumultuous Rift Valley. The great eastern wall of the Rift rises blue-grey in the distance on the other side, the valley stretching away as far as the eye can see to Lake Bogoria and beyond: through searing heat and dusty desert to Marigat, Baringo and ultimately to the cataclysmic volcanic cones that mark the southern shores of Lake Turkana.

Bogoria lies sixty kilometres from Nakuru at the foot of the Laikipia Escarpment, the sheer cliffs rising up more than 2,000 feet out of its eastern shores — a long narrow sheet of alkaline water coated with a sheen of flamingo. Its western shores are a torment of spurting cauldrons, hot springs that erupt out of the rocky ground.

Sunburst over the top edge of the Siracho Cliffs is spectacular. Painting the geysers a molten gold against the backcloth of the hundreds of flamingos, their pink feathers suddenly alive with gleaming liquid oranges and purples, the steaming, ever-rumbling gushers testify to the latent power beneath the surface that shaped the Rift in the tempest of creation.

Bishop Hannington camped around the lake in the 1890s on his way to Uganda, where he was murdered, and it was known as Lake Hannington until it was endowed, after Independence, with the name it had long been known by among the local communities. Harsh and arid, this magnificent country is now Bogoria National Reserve.

In 1987 a new lodge was being erected on the main entrance road, but Bogoria, hidden in its bowl beneath the cliffs, its steep rocky shores a mixture of reds and sere green, remains remote and rugged, its harsh beauty undefiled by development. A grove of giant fig trees dominates the southern shore, which become prolific with baboons when in fruit.

It was along this dry and dusty valley, becoming ever drier and more barren as you descend, that John Walter Gregory travelled in the 1890s to Baringo, a lacustrine paradise whose cool green shores provide an oasis in the enervating stamina-sapping heat of the Rift.

Baringo's shallow silt-stained waters, like those of Naivasha, are odd contrast to the rest of the Rift lakes. They are the only two freshwater lakes along the length of the Kenya section. Studded with islands, it sustains healthy populations of fish — tilapia — and crocodile and hippo.

The largest island, Ol Kokwe, is well settled, but the eastern promontory boasts one of Kenya's most delightful tourist retreats, Island Camp. Far from anything but the noisy silence of an African night — insects, frogs, water birds — a night spent here is therapeutic. No noise of man nor machine breaks the spell, and the stars above sparkle like diamonds. On the island's northern shores there are more hot springs,

121

Above: The maniacal scream of the tiny rock hyrax, magnified by the rock crevasses in which it lives, is one of nature's most terrifying sounds. Hyrax are the highest living creatures in Kenya, found at the edge of existence at around 14,000 feet on Mount Kenya's moorlands.

Opposite: In spate the waters of the Ewaso Ngiro plummet more than 230 feet over Thomson's Falls at the rate of a million litres a minute to vanish hundreds of kilometres downstream in the Lorien Swamp.

food, however, reflects the sylvan Highland beauty of its setting.

Two fine new roads lead out of Nyahururu — one northward down the steep gradient of the Marmanet Forest to the ranching town of Rumuruti, a major gateway to the northern deserts; the other south-east to Nyeri, with many dirt roads branching off across the Laikipia Plains.

Along this road is Solio Ranch, where the benevolent owners have devoted many acres to nursing a nucleus herd of Kenya's threatened rhinoceros so successfully that, in 1987, Kenya's Conservation and Wildlife Department began a major translocation operation — removing many of these creatures to specially created sanctuaries within national parks and reserves. This much-hunted creature may yet flourish again in the ancestral lands the species has roamed for more than sixty million years. In the 1980s the beast was on the brink of extinction. Yet the horn, which in 1987 fetched a market price of US$65,000 to make dagger handles in the Yemen and medicinal ingredients in the Far East, contains nothing more valuable than the keratin that makes up mankind's own fingernails.

Neither black nor white — the difference is one of semantics — the black rhinoceros is the smaller of the two species, weighing around 900 to 1400 kilograms. Average size of the front horn is between fifty and ninety centimetres; the back measures around fifty-three centimetres. With its relatively small feet, three toes on each hoof, and pointed prehensile upper lip, the black rhinoceros is a browser that used to be found anywhere from sea level up to the 11,000-foot contours of Kenya's mountains, from savannah to montane forest.

In a number of smaller reserves in Kenya, where wardens can keep a close guard over its movements, the species maintains a precarious hold on life. With a life span between thirty and forty years, the total number of rhinoceros throughout the world is now believed to be no more than 30,000.

The white rhinoceros, which derives its name from the Afrikaans word *weit*, meaning wide-mouthed, is a grazer, not a browser, and much more sociable and sedentary than its black kin, moving in gregarious groups. Much bigger, it weighs between 2,000 and 4,100 kilograms — making it the largest of all land animals after the elephant. In 1987, there was a flourishing group on Solio Ranch, but the only ones in national parks formed a small group in Meru National Park.

Even so, some rhinoceros still roam the Laikipia, where settlement schemes and co-operatives have rapidly segmented the former large-scale ranches, though some still exist. One vast ranching spread also serves, like Solio, as a private wildlife reserve — the 6,500 hectares of scrub savannah and thorn called Ol Pejeta. For many years it was the Kenya playground of armaments billionaire Adnan Kashoggi, but in the wake of the Iran arms deal, this was seized by the Kenya subsidiary of the giant Lonrho group in settlement of debts Kashoggi owed the conglomerate. He had already transferred his ownership of the Mount Kenya Safari Club to the group.

In 1984, film star Brooke Shields spent an idyllic day among the ranch's elephants and lions — one memorable moment came when a pride feasted on cattle meat in the back of the pick-up she was driving. Under

Above: Fourteen Falls, where the waters of the Athi River cascade downstream in the shadow of 7,041-foot-high Ol Doinyo Sapuk, near Thika.

Opposite: Thundering in a series of steps a thousand feet down a narrow gorge, the waters of an Aberdare trout stream turn into the magnificent Gura Falls.

Juja Farm at Thika, where guests would go pig-sticking; he also owned the Chiromo Forest in Nairobi, where the university campus now stands. He was an enormous man who made the Mountain of the Buffalo, Ol Doinyo Sapuk, his personal domain.

He died in 1921, and was buried high up the mountain's forested slopes, above the cascading roar of Fourteen Falls, where countless wild buffalo still roam in what is now a national park, to be joined later by his widow and their faithful servant, Louise Decker. In 1928, Lady MacMillan honoured her husband's memory by building Nairobi's MacMillan Library. Louise Decker's name also lives on in an old folks home in Nairobi.

MacMillan was a man of boundless spirit with a girth — 1.6 metres — to match. In a dispute over his land with Nairobi Municipal Council just before his death, he had his lawyer present his case with amazing clarity. But when the time came to cast the vote, the lawyer — who was also a councillor — raised his hand against, the sole objector.

Though now unprepossessing as a community, Thika boasts the world's third largest pineapple plantation, run by the Del Monte conglomerate. There's also a country club to the west of the town with rolling fairways and verdant greens for golf. In 1983, Queen Elizabeth II ate lunch here before driving on to Nyeri. The club is not far from the Blue Posts Hotel, built in the first decade of the century, close to the Chania waterfalls where Churchill camped during his African journey in 1907 — hoping to shoot a lion but, though he heard many, he was frustrated. With its heavy industries, it's odd to think that just ninety years ago this area of Kenya was as wild and thick with game as the Maasai Mara today.

Far from the amenities of town life, the settlers made their own recreations and Makuyu Country Club is the third of the three golf clubs in this region, set amid olive green coffee plantations not far from an abandoned sisal plantation.

It's on the borderline between the traditional lands of the Kikuyu and the Kamba, from which a rough road leads east to Kandara Valley in the northern lea of Kilimambogo. Ruggedly beautiful, the close-cropped crests of the once forested hills have combined with frequent drought to make this potentially productive area marginal land. The dirt road has turned to deep, fine-grained sand — a finger of the northern deserts only an hour's journey from the Kenya capital.

To the west, however, on the slopes of the Aberdares, the land is still bountiful. The mountain massif falls steeply away and many enchanted valleys, where flashing streams fat with trout dance down the hillside, have been cultivated by smallholders. Lured by the crisp, bracing air, open moorlands, gushing streams and rugged rock outcrops, Europeans were quick to settle these mountains. The scene's just as pastoral today — handsome open meadows stocked with fat herds of grazing sheep and cattle.

From Thika, a rugged dirt track follows the course of the Chania River through ancient forest. In the thickleaf canopy, the agile and beautiful black and white colobus monkeys leap from the branches, their coats extended like a parachute, in long, gliding swoops. Buffalo trample through the undergrowth. All this land is tended by rangers based at

136

Above: Saddlebill stork — bird of river, swamp and marsh.

Kimakia Forest Station. There's a log fishing cabin nearby, run by the Kenya Fisheries Department, and the brown trout stocked in these waters by Colonel Grogan in the first decade of the century are doughty fighters.

On the Kinangop salient, close to the Kimakia Forest, these waters flow into Sasamua Dam, Nairobi's first major water catchment scheme, built in the 1950s. North Kinangop is not much more than a few wood-and-tin-roofed houses, often isolated during the rains. South Kinangop boasts a tarred road and red-tiled service station.

Higher up, the views over the Rift are spectacular. Above, the clouds curl around the 12,815-foot-high rocky tor of the second highest point in the Aberdares, Kinangop. A stone cairn commemorates the first ascent by a European early in the century. Though it demands little mountaineering skill, it requires monumental stamina to reach the crown: the rarefied air at this height sucks the breath from the lungs with every stride.

From Kinangop the ground falls quickly away to the broad moorland plateau, which stretches north forty-six kilometres to Lesatima, forming the main bulk of the Aberdares National Park, established in 1948. Most of this lies above 10,000 feet, with one gate from the Naivasha side — up a rough rocky road that amazingly turns into tarmac near the top, laid in 1959 for the visit of Britain's Queen Mother — and several gates from Nyeri, Mweiga, and Pesi on the eastern face. For many, the Aberdare National Park is arguably Kenya's most beautiful.

Close to Nairobi and many major towns — Thika, Nakuru, Nyeri — the transition from city streets to the game-rich moors high above, for any visitor, from the city or abroad, is a profound experience. Frustratingly — yet to the benefit of its wild flora and denizens — the park is often inaccessible during the rains. Even in the dry season, the high altitude and rough trails make four-wheel drive virtually mandatory. But the delights are ample reward. Here are some of Kenya's most ancient forests, their gnarled and rheumy limbs like some fantasy from a Tolkien fable, often shrouded with clammy fingers of mist and decorated with Old Man's Beard, Spanish moss, whose wispy festoons dangle from every branch and leaf.

Alpine oddities include giant heather, tussock grass sometimes a metre or two deep, St. John's wort, lobelia and groundsel, grown to astonishing heights under the ultra-violet glare at this height on the Equator. The groundsel comes into flower only once in every twenty years or so. Kenya's mountain elephant — smaller than their lowland kin — plod their steady way through this undergrowth and the forests, carving trails that demonstrate, despite their bulk, their astonishing agility and nimble-footedness. These moorlands were the main strategic hideout of the Mau Mau freedom fighters. When the British tried to flush them out with bombing runs over the plateau, many a cave and many an impenetrable forest served their purpose. But unexploded bombs still occasionally turn up, a hazard to human and wildlife.

The park is a delight of rolling downs, open vistas, little dells, icy tarns, burbling streams and waterfalls: with Mount Kenya eighty kilometres away across the Laikipia, it forms Kenya's major watershed. Rivers from both massifs merge at Kiambere on the Mwea Plains to form

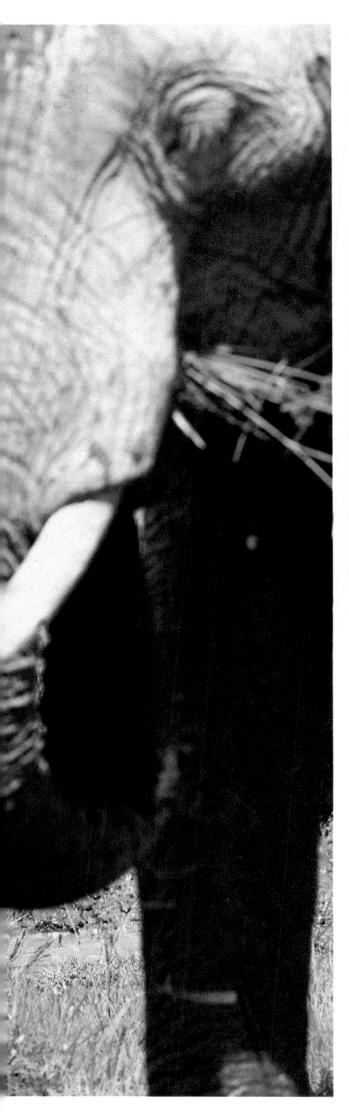

Left: Elephant and young in mud bath. Elephant are the only animal species known to disperse the bones of their dead or cover them with ground litter.

Below: Cape buffalo, most ferocious of Africa's Big Five when roused. Buffalo have killed more professional hunters than any other species.

the Tana, Kenya's longest and most powerful river.

Game here is little used to man's presence. Shy fawns and bucks come to within hand's reach but the lions have a well-earned reputation for ferocity. At one stage, after campers had been held in terror through the night, camping in the 767-square-kilometre park was suspended. One beast even attacked a Land Rover, shredding the tyres while the terrified passengers cowered inside.

Near one of the gates from Nyeri, there's a fishing camp with log cabin at around 10,000 feet. Both brown and rainbow trout flourish in the icy streams and some have been weighed in at seven kilos.

The moors are alive with buffalo, perhaps the fiercest of all African game when roused, and large antelope, as well as many melanistic species of lowland creatures. The high altitude and closeness to the Equator have turned their coats black. But there are some mythical beasts, too, including a spotted lion which has never been seen.

The roaring waters of Queen's Cave Waterfall — so called because Queen Elizabeth of Britain lunched here and the remains of the wooden pavilion testify to her visit — cascade into a small ravine that's like a fairy glade. You reach it by climbing down the cliff.

Another spectacular fall, Kenya's deepest, is the Gura. It plummets more than a thousand feet into an impenetrable ravine opposite the Karura Falls, which drop almost 900 feet to merge downstream into the Chania River. These waters, swaying like a pliant ribbon in the strong winds that gust along the Gorge, were filmed for a scenic essay in *Out of Africa*. All these natural wonders occur well above the Aberdare forest

belt, which begins around the 10,000-foot contour, giving way lower down, around the 8,000- and 7,000-foot contours, to the bamboo belt, and beyond that to lush, well-tended smallholdings of vegetables, tea and coffee, which gaze down on towns like Makuyu, Murang'a and Nyeri.

From Makuyu the railway twists and loops across these rolling foothills, in the eastern lea of the Aberdares and the Tana River to Murang'a, while a smooth new tarred road cuts across the plains below to Sagana, where it links up with the railway again. No other river in the world has been exploited for hydro-electric power in the same way as the Tana. In 1987 work was continuing on the seventh hydro-electric scheme along its upper reaches. The previous one — on the Sagana road — has created a forty-kilometre-long lake already used for fish farming and a waterfowl reserve and is to be developed as a marina.

The first was constructed downstream at Kindaruma, destroying forever the spectacle of Seven Forks — so named for the number of rivers which merged into the Tana — that plunged 450 foot in a roaring torrent of untapped power.

Just out of Murang'a at a place called Mugeka, there used to be a museum and an original fig tree, but they no longer exist. According to Kikuyu legend, God, *Ngai*, sits atop the twin peaks of the mountain they call Kirinyaga — place of brightness. It was he who ordered Gikuyu and Mumbi, the father and mother of all Kikuyu, to make their home at Mukuruene wa Nya-Gathanga — 'tree of the building site' — a grove of wild figs, a tree that, like Mount Kenya, is sacred to the Kikuyu people.

Above: Kenya's only white rhino are found at Meru National Park and at Solio Ranch on the Laikipia Plain. Second largest living land creature in the world, they dwarf their smaller kin, the black rhinoceros. Their name derives from the Afrikaans word, weit — *meaning wide-mouthed.*

Above: Pickwickian-like black and white colobus monkey, most beautiful of all Kenya's primates.

Here, affirms the tribe's genesis myth, Mumbi raised the nine daughters who were the matriarchs of the nine Kikuyu clans. Although to the casual observer the Kikuyu seems a deeply-embedded male chauvinist community along the lines of the Maasai — with whose culture the Kikuyu share many similarities — the tribe's culture is based entirely on matriarchal traditions.

The largest ethnic group in Kenya, numbering about four million in 1987, Kikuyu society is built around the family, often a large and extended unit, and the clan. Mothers guide husbands and sons with sound advice and chastising tongues. They inculcate girls into the ways of womanhood. Polygamy is natural, often loving. Once married, a woman lights a fire in the traditional three-stone hearth and must never allow it to go out. To do so would bring misfortune.

Goats are killed to propitiate tribal spirits, to remove curses and to provide omens for the future. On these often festive occasions, honey beer is brewed from honey, sugar water and the loofah-like fruit of the *muratina* tree. Fermented in a large vessel, set on a small pile of cattle dung by the glowing embers of the fire, *muratina* is traditionally decanted into a gourd and served in a cow horn always passed with the right hand around a circle of men. The women sit elsewhere during this formal, rigidly observed ritual. But in a salute to her supremacy it is the matriarch who receives the last of the gourd's contents.

The key to Kikuyu philosphy is land: what cattle are to the Maasai and the Samburu, land is to the Kikuyu — the only measure of wealth, prosperity, stability and happiness. It was the European settlers who alienated traditional Kikuyu lands — particularly those around Mount Kenya — and whose action gave rise to the Mau Mau rebellion, ultimately leading to Independence. This was ushered in under one of the most traditional yet progressive Kikuyu elders — Mzee Jomo Kenyatta, whose 1938 book, *Facing Mount Kenya*, was a firm justification of female circumcision and polygamy, both cardinal tenets of Kikuyu society.

If a youth is to be accepted as an adult member of Kikuyu society, male circumcision is necessary to move through a series of age-grades to an elderhood, which holds sway sometimes for as long as thirty years. Though deeply superstitious, Kikuyu society has embraced every innovation of western trade, industry and technology and often improved upon it.

There's something of the Scot about their ways and their character — thrifty, industrious, clever with their hands. They live in round thatched huts which they share with their livestock — as the Scots did four centuries ago. They brew a fine, colourless whisky, celebrate major occasions with the haggis, the boiled innards of the goat or sheep stuffed in gut skin, and dance a passable Highland reel of their own. Not surprisingly the kirk — the Presbyterian Church founded in Scotland by John Knox — is the strongest of Kikuyuland's secular faiths.

Muranga's Anglican church, St. James, was dedicated by the Archbishop of Canterbury as a memorial to the thousands of Kikuyu who died as the result of reprisal raids by the Mau Mau in the freedom war. It has a mural by a famous Kenya artist, Elimu Njau, which depicts both the nativity and the last supper — as well as the crucifixion of a

141

black Christ in a typical Murang'a landscape. Murang'a used to be called Fort Hall, after the British officer who commanded the garrison there and built a compound.

Richard Meinhertzhagen, an English officer, was based in Murang'a in the first decade of this century and led many a punitive expedition against the intractable Kikuyu for whom, nonetheless, he had many sympathies. He once evicted a white missionary, whose method of gaining female converts was to baptize them by sleeping with them.

The town stands on the brow of a cliff which plunges down to the Tana Valley. Now a new road cuts along the lower part of the cliff above the river to Nyeri, through countryside fat with farms. The old road and the railway roll out on the other side of town to Sagana to head north-west to Karatina — or north-east to Embu.

Some distance before Sagana a smooth new road also leads north-east, cutting through the Mwea National Reserve, a flush of brilliant green rice paddies, irrigated by the Tana waters, where wildfowling is allowed by permit, to the hill town of Embu. East of Mwea, the Tana cuts a green swathe through the sere and withered bushlands bordering Kamba territory, where the Mbeere community ekes out a fragile existence.

These 75,000 people, who share cultural and historic affiliations with the Embu, watched progress pass them by until recently. Living in close affinity with a broad range of wildlife — even a few elephant and rare rhino roam the arid plains — they still practise hunting. Their arrows, tipped with a virulent poison, are exceptionally well-made. They cultivate scrub patches with 'digging sticks' to grow millet and cowpeas to stave off famine, which is no stranger in these parts. The Tana's exploitation has brought them into the mainstream of Kenya national life and the new generations of Mbeere are poised to take a dramatic step from the nineteenth to the twenty-first century in one stride.

Embu's streets and houses straggle down the lower slopes of Mount Kenya. Above the town, flashing through the thick forest in their haste to greet the Tana, are some of Kenya's finest fly fishing rivers. Not for nothing is Embu's timbered, cottage-style hostelry known as the Isaak Walton Inn, after the grand seventeenth-century patron of English anglers who wrote *The Compleat Angler*. He would have delighted in the fat river bounty and forest landscapes above Embu.

But the extension of Girouard's 1913 'tramway' from Thika to Nanyuki between 1927 and 1930 passed Embu by. From Sagana the track clings to the north-west foothills of Mount Kenya, climbing to Karatina through a riot of fertile hill farms, lush with groves of juicy banana palms, vegetables, fruit, tea, coffee and flowers, all stepping down the hills in neat terraces, the swift waters of the Sagana River and its tributaries providing year-round irrigation.

An untidy, unkempt town, Karatina has no special claim to Kenya fame, except as one of the major strongholds of the Mau Mau movement during the freedom battle and threshold to what is arguably Kenya's most magnificent country: main gateway to both the Aberdares and Mount Kenya. During the dry season, the town is a swirl of dust, during the rains, a sea of mud. But its market is one of the most colourful in the country — a vivid splash of colourful cloths, grains, utensils, vivacious traders and buyers.

Above: Tharaka bee-keepers fashion hives by hollowing out the trunk of a tree. Famed also as drummers, the 12,000-strong Tharaka community fashion drums the same way, marking each with the emblem of their specific clan.

The rounded foothills of both the Aberdares and Mount Kenya merge here in a cluster of domed, forested crowns, many of them cleared and turned into tidy farms. The road from Karatina to Nyeri dips up and down like a twisting roller-coaster, fast-flowing streams running along the side.

Railhead never reached Nyeri. It veered northwards, through the forests between Karatina and the great sweep of the wheatlands on the western slopes of Mount Kenya, a landscape that fills the eye with images of breathtaking beauty amid crisp mountain air that fills the lungs like a charge of electricity. Trout streams leap down the mountain moorlands and through the forests. On one stretch you can flirt with your own trout and if successful hand it to the waiting chef to cook over the embers at the trout lodge.

It was at Sagana State Lodge — a gift of the colonial government to Princess Elizabeth and her consort, Prince Philip — on the morning of 6 February 1952, after a night watching game at Treetops, that the young girl was told she had become Queen of England following the death during the night of her father, King George VI.

Grief-stricken, she was escorted to a waiting car, the gentle breeze that soughed through the forest canopy singing its own lament, to be driven to Mweiga, where on the grass landing strip a DC-3 of East African Airways was waiting to fly the new Queen to Entebbe, Uganda, and then by another plane to Britain.

Not long after her visit the struggle for freedom erupted into one of the bloodiest guerilla wars in Africa.

Mau Mau forest fighters, skilled in bushcraft and forest lore, were active along the forest trails around Sagana and on Mount Kenya. As a result, the British herded hundreds of innocent Kikuyu — mothers and children, too — into vast concentration camps. One, at Gatu'ng'ang'a, was cut through the middle by the railroad. Now the land in the hills around belongs to these families. Climb the dirt road from Gatu'ng'ang'a, round the slope of the hill, and then up the steep road to its crest, and a scene of unsurpassed loveliness unfolds.

To the north-east, so close you feel you can touch them, rise the twin peaks of Mount Kenya, bathed in the soft, lambent flame of the dying, westering sun. To the north-west, a dark silhouette in the sudden close of day at the Equator, are the Aberdares. In front, to the north, young saplings straggle down the hillside, and neat avenues of coffee climb to the top of the hill beyond and over — and in the hazy distance stretches the infinite sweep of the Laikipia Plains.

To the east are more foothills and among them lurks Mountain Lodge. Near this lodge, set in a forest reserve at 7,000 feet, where elephants roam in abundance, an ancient tree at the roadside, with a cleft in its bole, was used as a Mau Mau mailbox. Urgent messages with notice of British troop movements were left in the cleft to be picked up by other forest units.

West of this lodge is Kiganjo. It was the closest the railway came to Nyeri, and for decades it was called Nyeri Station. Kiganjo is the base for Kenya's Police Training College, where many of the country's award-winning athletes first sprang to prominence. Each year graduates pass out to be deployed nationwide in the fight against crime.

143

When Meinhertzhagen visited Nyeri Hill in 1903 there was no visible community, but now it's one of Kenya's major towns and the administrative headquarters of Kenya's Central Province. The recently-built Provincial Headquarters occupies a large slice of Nyeri's beautiful cricket ground, but the golf course remains. Though visiting international cricket stars no longer perform in the shade of the flame trees, top golfers can still drive off Nyeri's farthest tee towards a startling image of ice-clad Mount Kenya. One of the tree-lined fairways runs parallel with the grounds of the Outspan Hotel, built by Eric Sherbrooke Walker and his wife Betty.

When they arrived in Nyeri in 1925, they were taken up a track alongside the Chania River to a patch of bare scrub facing Mount Kenya. Above the spot lay the Aberdares, and to the north the land plunged into the fern-shrouded gorge where the Chania boiled over the rocks. They could hardly believe their good fortune. 'The more we looked at it, the more strongly we felt it was the only place for our hotel.' The clubhouse, built of cedar bark shingles, and the golf course already existed, and the countryside all around was undergoing a transformation into coffee plantations, farmlands and sawmilling.

Sherbrooke Walker bought seventy acres of land from the colonial government and set about building the hotel: four bedrooms with water pumped up from the Chania. They offered a bottle of champagne for the best suggestion for a name for the hotel and neighbour Grace Barry, a sawmiller, suggested the Outspan — 'where at the end of the day's journey, the traveller outspans the weary oxen'.

Nyeri already had one hotel — the White Rhino, built by a trio of aristocrats — Berkeley Cole, Lord Cranworth and Sandy Herd. Both still exist, and the Outspan has mellowed and grown graceful through the years. When the founder of the World Scout movement, Lord Baden-Powell, the hero of Mafeking, who Sherbrooke Walker had served as Scout Commissioner and private secretary, visited his old aide in 1935 he fell in love with the 'wonderful views over the plains to the bold snow peaks of Mount Kenya'.

Two years later — ordered by his doctor in England to rest — he retired to the cottage on the hotel grounds which was built for him and his wife Olave. His house in Britain was called Pax — for Peace — and in a neat pun, a blend of Latin and Swahili, he christened his Nyeri home Paxtu.

When he died on 8 January 1941, he was buried in the Nyeri cemetery, where his grave and his last home have long been a pilgrimage shrine for Scouts and Guides from all over the world. In 1973 the scout movement held its 24th conference in Kenya, and in 1987 the Guides held their twenty-sixth world conference in the same country. On both occasions delegates paid tribute to their founding father at Baden-Powell's graveside.

Treetops was the creation of the Sherbrooke Walkers. Betty wanted a Wendy-style tree house inspired by the J. M. Barrie play, *Peter Pan*. Its first recorded visitors — in a two-room house perched precariously in a fig tree — stayed there in November 1932. Twenty years later, when Princess Elizabeth was escorted through the game infested forest to climb the ladder into the tree, she followed a distinguished list of royalty and celebrities — Tsar Ferdinand of Bulgaria, the Duke and Duchess of

Above: Meru dancer. Close kin of the Kikuyu, the million-strong Meru farm the fertile north-eastern slopes of Mount Kenya.

Above: Kikuyu matriarch. Largest of Kenya's ethnic communities, the four-million-strong Kikuyu are composed of nine clans, established, says Kikuyu folklore, by the nine daughters of Mumbi, the mother of all the Kikuyu.

Gloucester, Mr and Mrs Neville Chamberlain, and Earl Mountbatten. By then it had expanded to four rooms, but in 1954 it was burned down by the Mau Mau. Its replacement was finished — on a site opposite the original fig tree — in 1957 with 'seven wash basins and water closets'. Set in a salient of the Aberdares National Park, it grew considerably in the years between, and now accommodates almost eighty guests. It's a never-to-be-forgotten experience as darkness descends and the floodlights bathe the salt lick and waterhole below and the elephants amble in to drink. For many it's the definitive Kenya experience.

Treetops — given the royal accolade in November 1983 by the Queen's sentimental homecoming to the spot where she became Queen — remains unique. Though Nyeri and Kiganjo are just around the corner, this is authentic, wilderness Africa. A deep, large moat guards the perimeter of this spur of the park from the surrounding coffee farms and smallholdings — keeping the elephants in and the people out. Its only equals are the Ark, a more recent innovation higher up the Aberdares, where the bongo, a large but nocturnal forest antelope, is sometimes seen, and Mountain Lodge on the slopes of Mount Kenya above Kiganjo. Both offer considerably more space and comfort, but neither can boast that there a princess became Queen.

From Kiganjo, through Naro Moru to Nanyuki, the land on either side of the railroad is high, wide and handsome — to the west the Laikipia Plains, to the east the rolling moorland shoulders of Africa's second highest mountain. The twin peaks of Mbatian and Nelion crown one of the world's highest national parks, 704 square kilometres of forest, moorland, rock and ice. With its many ridges, radiating like the spokes of a wheel, the bulk of Mount Kenya straddles the Equator. Though its highest point lies seventeen kilometres to the south, the Equator cuts across the northern shoulders at a height of 11,000 feet.

Kenya is regarded as the perfect model of an Equatorial mountain. Nineteenth-century European geographers dismissed the idea of snow on the Equator as ridiculous. But forty years after Krapf's first sighting Thomson's delight at his discovery was lyrical. 'Through a rugged and picturesque depression in the range [Aberdares] rose a gleaming snow-white peak with sparkling facets which scintillated with the superb beauty of a colossal diamond. It was in fact the very image of a great crystal or sugar loaf.' Batian and Nelion, in fact, are the remains of a gigantic eroded plug that once thrust another 10,000 feet and more into the sky. Its Kikuyu name is derived from Kere Nyaga, 'White Mountain'.

The first Europeans to venture to any heights on the mountain were Count Samuel Teleki von Szek and Ludwig von Hohnel, who followed much of Thomson's epic route in their 1887 travels and went on to discover Lake Turkana, which they named Rudolf. The two Austrians explored the moorlands 3,000 feet beneath the peaks. Twelve years later, the great Victorian alpinist Sir Halford Mackinder made it to the summit, but so remote was Kenya in those days the significance of his achievement was underrated. In 1929, Eric Shipton, one of the first of Britain's Himalayan specialists, made the second recorded ascent.

Perhaps the most unusual assault, however, was the one made by three Italian prisoners of war interned at Nanyuki during the 1940s. They broke out of the camp to climb the mountain equipped only with the label from a tin of canned meat as their map.

Hunger and the alpine weather overcame the runaways, whose failure makes the account of their adventures in the book *No Picnic on Mount Kenya* all the more dramatic than success might have been.

Their exploit over, they calmly returned to camp to resume their confinement. In 1987 a major Hollywood movie maker was preparing to shoot a feature film in Kenya based on the book.

The main park gate is reached by crossing over the railway and then the main road along a track from Naro Moru, a sleepy farming settlement with a fishing and climbing lodge set on the banks of the trout stream from which the village takes its name. The dirt road to the Naro Moru park gate climbs slowly at first, through grasslands and smallholdings, and then cuts through a forest reserve, climbing more steeply to the gate. It's set at around 8,000 feet on a ridge with deep valleys on either side that plunge down to the humid bamboo belt, lush and sweltering, the tracks a boggy morass where game darts through the bush.

Along the saddle of the ridge the ancient forest giants cast a canopy of shade, but the air is noticeably cooler. Lovely black and white colobus monkeys leap from one branch to another while beneath them morose-faced, belligerent buffalo glare through thickets. Few sights are more graceful than a colobus on the move. As it leaps through the topmost levels of the forest with its fur and tail spread out like a vibrant cape, it appears to glide. But in silhouette it is distinctly pot-bellied, a caricature-like Pickwickian figure.

Colobus differ from most monkeys in two respects. They have four fingers but no thumb, and they spend virtually their entire lives above the ground. Rarely, if ever, do they come down to earth. Not many creatures can match their climbing ability or their leap — as much as thirty metres. And for monkeys they are unusually silent, uttering no sound for hours on end. Their lovely coat is much sought after — the colobus skin is the badge of office of senior elders of the Kikuyu — and has put their existence in jeopardy.

Beyond the forest, above 10,000 feet, the road ends at the Met Station, leaping-off point for moorland walks and climbing expeditions. This quick access to high altitude has its risks for lowland visitors. Most of the National Park lies above the 11,500-foot contours, and trekkers are walking at between 12,000 and 14,000 feet. Climbers venture even higher — often within the space of hours. With insufficient acclimatization, pulmonary and cerebral oedema — fluid on the lungs and brains — is endemic on this mountain. As the rarefied air cuts down the oxygen which produces vital red blood cells, symptoms vary from breathlessness, nausea, disorientation and slurred speech. Without swift attention the result is often fatal.

It seems odd that this part of the earth, so close to the sun, should also be one of the coldest. But the sun's rays become warmest where the air is thickest — boosting the invisible atoms of atmosphere, thus causing them to collide more often and create more warmth. Where the air is thinner, the atoms are fewer: the collisions which give off heat occur less frequently. At night on Mount Kenya it's bitterly cold — and, even during the day, clouds sweeping beneath the sun can cause a 30° Fahrenheit temperature variation on Mount Kenya's moorlands and icy

peaks.

Above: A shrine for Scouts and Guides worldwide — Lord Baden-Powell's grave in Nyeri's St. Peter's Churchyard.

Above: Britain's Queen Elizabeth II walks the spot where in 1952 she spent the night in Treetops, only to be told in the morning that her father, King George VI, had died during the night and that she was now Queen.

Little grows at its extreme heights — just a few lichen cover the exposed rock. But in the high valleys, some of the world's most spectacular mountain plants flourish — 'water-holding cabbages' or 'ostrich plume plants' are actually giant groundsel, an astonishing mutation of a tiny alpine plant here growing, as on the Aberdares, Mount Elgon and the Cheranganis, to astonishing heights. When the leaves die, they remain attached to the plant like an overcoat keeping out much of the cold.

The lobelias grow even higher than the twenty-foot-high groundsel — up to twenty-seven feet — their hairy, grey leaves dotted with tiny blue flowers. It looks like a grotesque furry giant, but the wrapping seals out the frost at night. Another grows closer to the ground in the shape of a huge rosette filled with water. At night this freezes over but the ice wards off deeper penetration, thus protecting the central bud.

These plants mark the extreme range of wildlife. The only permanent residents at this altitude are the rock hyrax, a distant cousin of the elephant no bigger than a rabbit, which live off the lobelia leaves. In fact, superficially they look like a guinea pig. The rock hyrax — its savannah equivalent is the tree hyrax — moves with astonishing agility across these precipitous rocks. Its sole has semi-elastic, rubber-like pads which provide a sure grip on all inclines in all conditions.

The moorlands at around 11,000 feet start with a heath zone of *Erica arborea*, a weirdly-shaped bush, often as large as a tree and covered with moss and lichen, giving way to the tussock grass and a rich profusion of everlasting helichrysums, gladioli, delphiniums and 'red-hot pokers' — a   147 riot of unusual flora. Buffalo and elephant sometimes roam the moorlands where lion remain permanent residents, and eland and zebra have been seen occasionally at around 14,000 feet at the base of the peaks. In 1929, the year of Shipton's ascent, Carr's Road from the Meru Gate became the highest motor track in Africa when a Model T Ford climbed to above 14,000 feet.

More than thirty jewel-like lakes encircle Mount Kenya's rocky spires, including the Curling Pond beneath the Lewis Glacier and Lake Michaelson. One of these was the location for what may well have been the highest underwater exploration ever undertaken when a group of aqualung *aficionados* lugged their oxygen cylinders up to its shores and plunged to the bottom.

But it's for the climbs on its cliffs and rock faces that Kirinyaga is renowned. Though much lower, many claim these are as testing as the major Himalayan climbs — a challenge of couloirs, ice-cliffs, secondary peaks, cornices and sheer rock walls. The sun melts the snow swiftly. Firm ice and snow become treacherous lips of slush in hours.

For this reason all climbing is best done in the two dry seasons — January to early March and July to early October. The ridge between Batian and Nelion, above 17,000 feet, is known as the Gates of Mist. Here, early in the morning, the great savannah plains of Kenya stretch out far-distant for hundreds of kilometres. Slowly a finger of mist materializes in the crisp air as the sun begins to warm the sky — a phantom entrail that drifts forward as the breeze strengthens to clamp its clammy fingers on the ridge. Within minutes vision is obliterated and the cold is piercing. Now the wind begins to gust, playing hymnals in the organ vaults of the cliff walls beneath that sing of faiths older than mankind's.

The railhead stopped beneath Mount Kenya's north-western face, at Nanyuki in 1930. A ranching town, it became famous when William Holden made his African home in the plush Mount Kenya Safari Club, ninety acres of immaculately landscaped gardens, lush with colourful tropical blooms, gazing up at Mount Kenya. The Club, which boasts a golf course and heated swimming pool, was regarded in Holden's day as the world's most exclusive club, with founding members like Winston Churchill. It was treated as a 'get-away-from-it-all' retreat by Holden's Hollywood cronies. After he died, it was bought by Adnan Kashoggi, who later sold it to the giant Lohnro conglomerate.

But Holden's memory is enshrined in the living legacy of the William Holden Wildlife Education Centre just outside the club, funded by Americans like President Ronald Reagan. It's administered by his old partner Don Hunt, who runs the Mount Kenya Game Ranch, which he and Bill founded, and film star Stefanie Powers, who shared Holden's love of Kenya and its wildlife.

Though a survey was carried out, plans to extend the railway line to Meru, on the eastern slopes of Mount Kenya, never materialized. Nonetheless, this bustling town, reached along the circular road which leaves Nanyuki and travels through Timau, is one of Kenya's fastest growing.

It was once remote from mainstream Kenya because of the atrocious

road, but in 1983, high up on the mountain, British engineers built a smooth new highway from Embu to complete the circular mountain route, with viaducts spanning dizzying ravines and gorges.

High above the town on the mountain slopes are forests and lakes sacred to the Meru tribe, close kin of the Embu and Kikuyu. Beneath it the lush lands proliferate with bounteous produce. A spur of the mountain highway leads to Meru National Park, one of Kenya's loveliest, providing a remarkable range of environments and rich with elephant and lion. At the elegant, rondavel-style Meru Mulika Lodge, the living canvas of nature's masterpiece is rich with colour and perspectives: lion stalking prey, giraffe ambling by, while through the trees and in the sky above, myriad birds in a profusion of startling blues, reds, yellows and pastels, skim by searching for bees, insects and nectar.

It was here that George and Joy Adamson brought Boy, son of Elsa, to rehabilitate him to the wild and hunting. Here, too, Joy trained Pippah the cheetah back to her wild ways. Pippah's death is marked by a simple cairn in the riverine forest. Here the mighty Tana boils and bubbles over Adamson's Falls, the last of the major rapids and cataracts it encounters before broadening out on its stately journey to the Indian Ocean.

Octogenarian George, now widowed, lives some kilometres downstream, in the remote Kora National Reserve, a place of wild fascination to all who visit it or him. In the early 1980s, a British research expedition set up their camp near that of the author of *My Pride and Joy* and discovered what made this fascinating part of the world tick.

Leonine in aspect and character, George relishes his isolated refuge from the hectic pressures of twentieth-century life — a benign and lively old man who looks twenty years younger. He shared his existence with his brother Terence until he died in 1986 and a younger disciple, Tony Fitzjohn.

Like our earliest forefathers, George Adamson, with his great mane of silver hair and shaggy beard, has spent most of his life in close affinity with the wilderness and its creatures, and counts the wealth of his experiences more valuable than any material treasures. Out there in the fastness of still wild Africa, far from the city streets and crowded suburbia of the western world, George has found something elusive, long sought by millions but denied to them — a sense of belonging and tranquility. Perhaps here in this magical land, in the roots which our ancestors abandoned so long ago, he has discovered the true meaning of life.

6 · Land of Milk and Honey

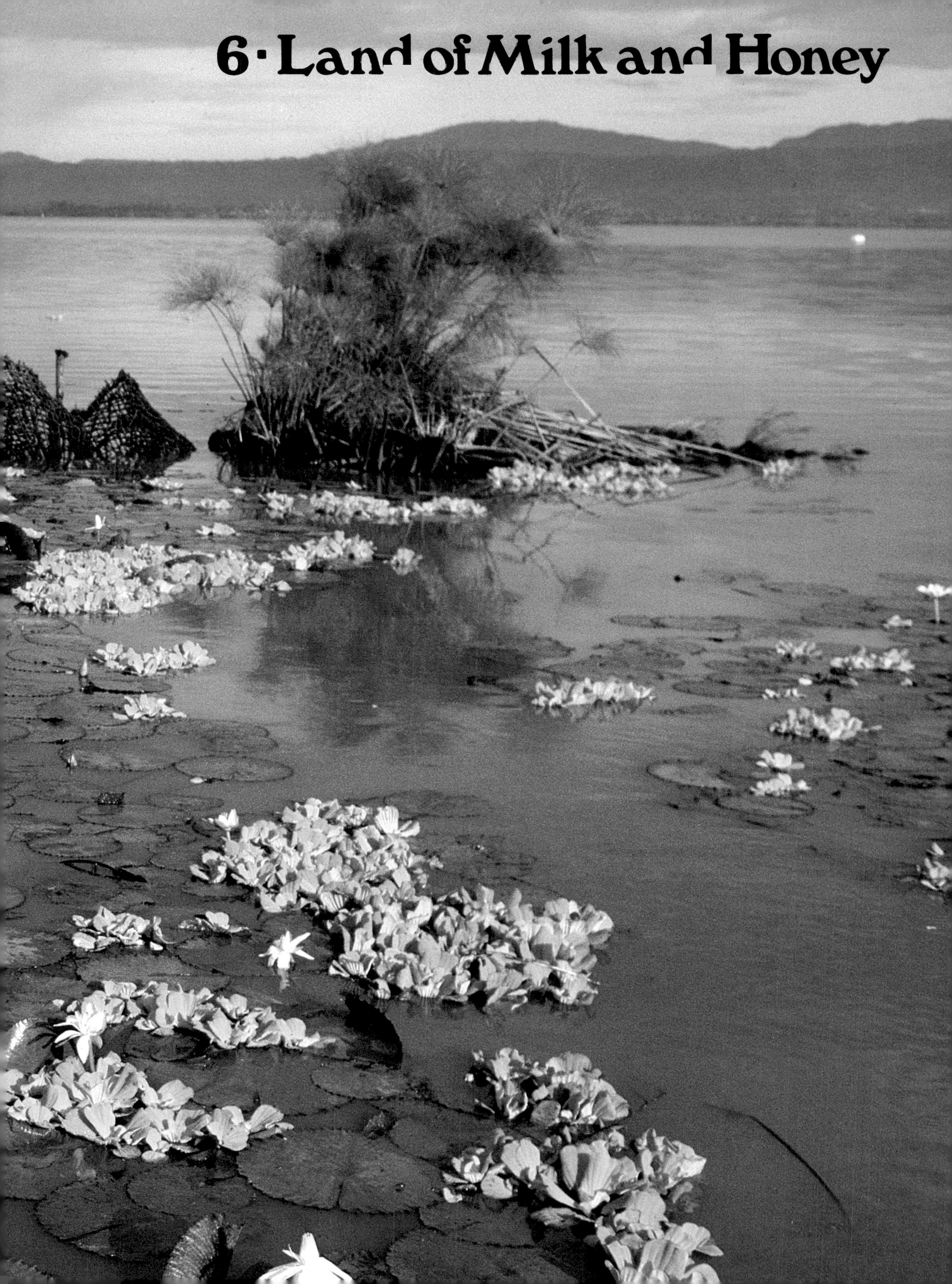

It was at Nakuru that Preston began to scent the west. The route of the initial survey would have taken him through the formidable Eldama Ravine, on to the Uasin Gishu plateau and across the Equator, but a new route — shorter by 160 kilometres — had been found over the Mau Escarpment, whose heights reach more than 10,000 feet above sea level.

To reach that daunting peak, however, the rail gangs first had to climb something like 3,000 feet in the space of sixty kilometres through fertile hills, land ideal for farming and sheep rearing, the first place being the handsome pastures around Njoro, where Delamere established his first Kenya estate, still a pleasant farm town noted for the excellence of the cheeses which the region produces.

Then it was around the folds of the contours to Elburgon, the dales and downs so reminiscent of a refined and purified English landscape, to Molo, where the grass is evergreen and a timbered roundhouse theatre remarks the brief tenancy of the European settlers who shaped the highest golf course in the Commonwealth — 8,500 feet — at the Highlands Hotel. Nothing exemplifies the British capacity for nostalgia better than this half-timbered rustic hostelry complete with skittle alley which could have been transposed straight from a fifteenth-century Elizabethan English village. Only the crackling log fires and crisp night air announces its Highland location.

In the event, a few kilometres beyond Molo, at its highest point, a height of 8,700 feet, the track cut through the great ancient stands of forest before its long descent to the humid Nyanza Plains and the shores of Lake Victoria. To reach the summit, however, required twenty-seven viaducts.

Preston built them of timber until steel arrived from the American Bridge Company in the USA. They curve and twist in a riotous elegance of trellises that span sparkling streams, deep ravines, and gentle valleys, enhancing rather than detracting from the beauty of the landscapes. So pure is the air of the Mau highlands that the first lick of paint on these viaducts weathered until 1967 before, finally, they needed another coat!

From the summit, this great massif sloped gently down for 6,000 feet to the lush, humid shores of Lake Victoria. All along the great ridge, the landscapes and climate were temperate and gentle — idyllic counterpoint to the harsh heat and wildlife of the savannahs and deserts now far away.

With the same kind of nostalgia so evident at Molo, in 1899, Londiani, the first stage in the line after the Mau, was declared the future capital of British East Africa — which then included Uganda — by Sir Harry Johnston, a Special Commissioner for Uganda, after he visited these tranquil meadows and forests. Later, however, it was discovered that the site was liable to flooding, and so another site was chosen near Molo. That, too, never came into existence. Today Londiani's straggling streets of timber and stone houses, rolling fields and wooded copses, remain a sleepy rural retreat of no more than 4,000 souls far from the hectic bustle and noise of Nairobi, the air as cool and exhilarating as a glass of champagne.

Railhead's arrival at Londiani coincided with the first wave of Voertrekkers, South African Europeans of Dutch descent, to Kenya. Their eyes were set covetously on the fertile lands atop the Uasin Gishu

Preceding pages: Luo fisherman places a maze basket trap at a Lake Victoria river mouth. Second largest freshwater lake in the world, Victoria's 68,800 square kilometres of water reap rich bounties of fish for the Luo and other communities who live on its Kenya shores.

152

Above: One of many caves on Kenya's moorland massif, 14,178-foot-high Mount Elgon, where elephant come to dig for salt. One such cave, Kitum, is said to have been the inspiration for Rider Haggard's adventure classic about the Queen of Sheba, She.

plateau across rugged unmarked country: along the top of the escarpment, where trails had to be hacked out of the thick forest and the ox-wagons, known as outspans, soon became bogged down in the torrential rains. The town they built, Eldoret, was for many years called simply Sixty-Four — being the distance from Londiani.

Strong breezes blow all day in the Equatorial highland forests of Kenya. The mountain ranges are alive with movement, the great canopies of the forest giants swaying and bending in a choreography of restless stillness. The cedars, blue gums, conifers, olives and oaks acrest the Mau Summit are an ocean of motion. They stand 9,000 feet above sea level, gazing down on the lush fertile plains of Kenya's sugarbowl that ranges the shores of Lake Victoria, one of the world's great freshwater lakes. All this land is encircled by a half moon of mountains and hills to form the great amphitheatre, which steps down, in a series of tiers, to Victoria.

Kericho and Kisii lie on the western slopes of the Mau, beyond which, fenced off by the Soit Olol Escarpment at the western extremity of the Maasai Mara, lie the moist, tropical plains of south-western Kenya. The verdant Nandi Hills form the centre-stand of the arena, while to the north-west rises the great massif of 14,178-foot-high Mount Elgon. As the fish eagle flies, it is just ninety-five kilometres from the Mau massif to the lake — a brief journey in time but, in the perspective of the contrasting landscapes, a journey through many different worlds. It is the least visited yet most populous and productive region of Kenya and, were it not for the coral coast and the game-rich savannahs in the south and north, would be a prime tourist attraction.

Few inland seas measure up to Lake Victoria's proportions. Its 68,800-square-kilometre surface — of which Kenya claims only 3,785 square kilometres — makes it the world's second largest freshwater lake, and the third largest of all lakes, exceeded in size only by Russia's Caspian

153

Sea and Lake Superior in North America. It creates a unique climate for Kenya's western regions, where the humidity is often drenching. As the sun sucks out the water, the cold air streams from the north pile up on the mountain ramparts which surround it. The result is heavy and consistent rainfall.

Above the western Mau, heralded almost always by bright, sunny mornings, lightning flashes and thunder rumbles nearly every day of the year in the late afternoon. Such equal amounts of rain and sunshine combine with the rich loams of these hills to make Kericho, Kisii and the Nandi Hills the most perfect tea growing region in the world. The old trail from Londiani, the nearest station to Kericho, cut through the thick forest lands of the Ondiek hunting and gathering group. Soon the giants fell to the woodsman's axe and in their place the hardy tea bush took firm root.

In 1987, Kericho's high plateau with its gentle hills was moulded with a mantle of brilliant green: plantations established as long ago as the 1920s were still yielding prolific high quality harvests of the little leaf that refreshes. Kenya tea has earned a reputation equal to that of its coffee: the *crème de la crème* of all teas. Such tea fetches premium prices at the regular Mombasa tea auctions.

To the harvests, culled from the plantations around Limuru, Kericho and the Nandi Hills, has been added the leaf produced through Kenya's unique smallholder scheme begun at Independence in 1963. By the 1980s, Kenya was the world's third largest producer of tea and the second largest exporter.

Above: Colourful fishing canoes on the shores of Lake Victoria. Though Kenya claims only one-tenth of its surface waters, Kenyan rivers provide much of the source of the Nile's intake.

Above: Kipsigis girl. One of the Kalenjin tribal communities, she wears the distinctive initiation dress of blackened skins.

Immaculately maintained, the curves, rhombs, cubes and triangles of these plantations — intercut with roads — create an astonishing panorama of nature manicured to man's concept of order and design. While coffee left wild is a tree which grows to giant heights and soon becomes jungle, tea is a bush. Its capacity to become tangled and unkempt is just as prolific, however, and it demands constant attention and pruning. But their strong roots hold the precious soil together and the thick green foliage continues to encourage the precipitation which the ancient forests demanded as their libation from the weather gods.

As befits the country's tea capital, Kericho is one of the tidiest towns in Kenya, laid out in neat patterns that reflect the ordered geometry of the tea plantations around its compact square. Where it drops down the escarpment south-west of Kericho, the road rises and falls along the curve of the hills, bending around great sweeps of rich and fertile farmland lush with sugar cane, maize fields and banana groves: a living pastoral canvas worthy of any of the great masters.

Kisii, the centre of the Gusii people, straggles without rhyme or reason down a steep hillside: a bustling, entrepreneurial town where trader and farmer vie with each other in their non-stop enterprise.

As fertile as the lands they till for bountiful crops of bananas, vegetables and fruit, along with their Bantu kin — the Luhyia, who occupy the lower slopes of the Nandi Hills — the Gusii are Kenya's most fecund community: so fecund in fact that they promise to break all known birth rate statistics. At 700 people to the square kilometre, the community has one of the highest population densities in Kenya — and the highest birth rate in the world. It's well above the national average of four per cent. Indeed, from a figure of one million in the 1979 population census, their numbers increased dramatically by 1987.

They also have a sadder statistic: the price they pay for the harvest of goodness the land yields. No region in Africa is so prone to lightning strike as these seemingly innocent hills. Indiscriminately, these periodic thunderbolts strike tree, house, school and farm building during the afternoon storms, often sending shock waves of horror and sympathy through the rest of the country when — as in the 1980s — more than twenty school children fell dead after a flash struck the tin roof of their classroom.

In the 1980s the Gusii were one of Kenya's most progressive communities — while preserving valued traditions. They have long been the most artistic of Kenyan ethnic groups. Elkana Ongesa's modern masterpieces, carved from the malleable pink and white soapstone quarried out of these hills, adorn UNESCO headquarters in Paris and offices in America. These quarries lie around the village of Tabaka — providing almost the entire world with this fine, elegant and delicately hued sculpting material. White is the softest, a rich roseate the hardest. Wherever you go, families are busy crafting the raw stone into chess pieces, eggs, and decorative shapes for home and office: ashtrays, wine glasses, candlesticks and so forth. It all finds its way to the vendors in Kenya's main tourist centres, where visitors snap up these little works of art to carry home.

For centuries, too, the Gusii's sensitive supple hands and fingers have deftly wielded the scalpel without formal training but with all the skill of 155 a modern surgeon. Practitioners carry out delicate trepanning operations on their patients to relieve headaches and mental illness — tapping a small hole in the skull to relieve the pressures causing the ailment — with such skill that they have earned mention in medical journals and the merit of a television documentary.

Traditionally, the country's sixth largest ethnic group is split into many clans, each of which forms a semi-independent local community. Heads of family used to judge minor social offences, invoking powerful curses as a final measure of disapproval. More serious crimes went before a council of elders. Soon after the arrival of the railway, this traditional democracy underwent severe pressures.

By 1905 European administrators and settlers, with their alien ideas of law and order, had enraged the community. Defying British imperial might, their army of spearsmen massed to hurl themselves — like the heroic Indians of America — at the rotating barrels of a lone Gatling gun, to be scythed down in their hundreds. In 1908, after a British official was speared, more massacres took place: as the Gusii fled they were mown down ruthlessly. Villages and fields were razed and the punitive force of the British spared none. Churchill, fresh from his African journey, was appalled. He cabled from Whitehall questioning the need to kill defenceless people on such 'an enormous scale'. The result left Gusii society in shreds — and yet in 1987, no trace of bitterness remained. The Gusii surely rank among the friendliest in a country where every community accords stranger and guest equal measures of friendship and hospitality.

Not far from the town, on the Kisumu Road, a sheer escarpment falls almost a thousand feet, giving breathtaking views of Lake Victoria. But it's to the south of Kisii that some of Kenya's most rewarding but least-visited landscapes and cultures lie. For the adventurous there's the winding road south-east to Kilkoris, where intrepid travellers try the often impassable dirt road over the Soit Olol escarpment to the Maasai Mara. Most stay on the main road, however, through Migori to the Tanzanian border, or turn off along the dusty trails that lead to the remote unspoilt beaches and fishing villages on the shores of Lake Victoria.

In the high hills above these shores live the Kuria community who, from time immemorial, have celebrated life with song and dance. In their traditional folk dances the men are weighed down with grotesque clogs — as much as eighteen centimetres thick — moving in unison to the rhythmic beat of the drums opposite a group of swaying, grass-skirted, topless girls.

Made up of seventeen clans, the Kuria trace their origins back to both the Gusii and the Abagumba communities. Their lands, like so many, were divided during colonial times by the unconcerned bureaucrats in Europe, who sliced up Africa like a loaf of bread — one slice for Britain, another for Germany, and so on — and though the majority of the Kuria live in Kenya, there are more than 100,000 in Tanzania.

Wedding arrangements are often made while a youngster is still at her mother's breast — for the groom, a protracted wait which he may have to endure for two decades or more before, in a series of elaborate ceremonies, he finally takes the chosen one as his bride.

156

Above: A young Bok boy after circumcision, member of a Kalenjin group known collectively as the Sabaot that lives on the slopes of Mount Elgon.

Above: Colourful Luo dancer. Migrating south along the Nile centuries ago, this agriculturalist Nilotic community quickly adapted to fishing and settled the shores of Lake Victoria.

Their closest kin, the Suba fisherfolk, live beneath the Kuria Hills on the shores and islands of Lake Victoria — from Tanzania in the south to Homa Bay in the north — and have a reputation as ferocious hippo hunters.

Although the railway never reached these parts, its arrival at Kisumu, further north along the lake coast, brought these remote villages and communities — Kehancha, on the wide sweep of Karungu Bay is one of the pearls — within the ambit of Britain's colonial administration.

Even before the railhead reached Victoria, boats assembled on the shore had started exploring the coastline. Though humid and malarial, Victoria's southern Kenya shore is a fascination of towering bluffs, great peninsulas, and islands. Kenya Railways marine division operates regular scheduled steamer services all along the coast, though the days when it was possible to take a seven-day luxury cruise around Lake Victoria — 3,720 feet above sea level — have long gone. But the majesty of this coastline remains — to be savoured from the deck of the smaller passenger vessels cruising these busy waterways.

From Mungeri Bay, the 7,450-foot-high Gwasi Hills rise almost 4,000 feet, the highest point in this region, to form the western boundary of the little-known Lambwe Valley National Reserve which, in the north, is bounded by the volcanic plugs of the Ruri Hills and to the north-west by the Gembe Hills. Its eastern border is formed by the Kanyamuia Escarpment. Always hot, infested with tsetse fly, Lambwe is one of the least developed and most natural of Kenya's game sanctuaries. Though the tsetse are fatal to man and his herds, wild game flourishes where they live, and here roam oribi, the rare Jackson's hartebeest and a colony of roan antelope, one of the most graceful antelopes: their only threat the stealthy leopards which haunt this dense scrubland.

For many these creatures are the most beautiful of Kenyan cats. Much smaller than lion, their sandy fur is covered with exquisite dark rosettes. Leopards move mainly at night and only rarely — except these days in the Mara and Amboseli — are seen during the day, resting up in the branches of a shady acacia. Superb hunters, they prefer to kill without stalking their prey — in an ambush by leaping from a tree and seizing the victim's neck or throat. They make their kill last long. What they cannot eat immediately, they haul up into a tree out of reach of scavengers. By this careful husbandry, they monopolize the kill, even though towards the end the meat is putrefied and rancid. The species has the same vocal mechanism as the lion but their roar, a grunting cough, sounds like a wood saw. It's often heard in undisturbed Lambwe Valley and occasionally a leopard will sneak out of its territory and raid the nearby shambas.

In cluttered and untidy Homa Bay town, with its rough roads and lone jetty, the fear is not of leopard but of the Lake Victoria crocodiles, which every now and then haul themselves off the beach to crawl into the downtown area — to the consternation and alarm of citizens going about their everyday business. Despite its unkempt appearance, Homa Bay is the administrative centre of a large area of Nyanza Province.

Take the steamer out of Homa Bay and you'll enter the Mbita Passage at the neck of the Kavirondo Gulf — the long inlet that leads to Kisumu — which passes between the mainland and Rusinga Island, birthplace of the late Tom Mboya, who was brutally assassinated in Nairobi in the 1960s.

One of Kenya's founding fathers, Mboya was one of the most outstanding and promising politicians of Africa's first generation of Independence statesmen. He lies buried here, on a rocky windswept shore, in a fine mausoleum, which is devoted to his life's work with memorabilia and artefacts of his life. His epitaph, like the man and his career, is an inspiration:

> *Go and fight like this man fought*
> *Who fought for mankind's cause*
> *Who died because he fought*
> *Whose battles are still unwon*

That cause to which he dedicated his life may well have had its very earliest beginnings on Rusinga Island. It was here that Mary Leakey, matriarch of Kenya's indomitable fossil-hunting family, uncovered the crumbling skull of *Proconsul africanus*, a primitive anthropoid ape which lived on Rusinga three million years ago. Even more outstanding, the earliest of the fossil remains uncovered on this dusty, bleak, eroded island — bridged by a controversial causeway in the 1980s — dates back seventeen million years.

Neighbouring Mfangano Island is more fertile and less visited, ruled by a three-man police squad and the local chiefs, and also a centre of prehistory with some ancient rock paintings. The islanders practise their own form of prehistoric fishing — casting kerosene lamps out from the shore after sundown and hauling them slowly inshore, luring squirming shoals of dagga, Victoria's freshwater shrimp and a much-loved delicacy, to their nets.

North of Homa Bay rises the gaunt crown of Homa Mountain, beneath which lime is quarried for Kenya's building industry and other manufacturing processes. The 5,745-foot-high mountain forms the centrepiece of a great rounded peninsula. Frequent thunderstorms play around its peak — jagged lightning streaking down through indigo night to play upon Victoria's wind-lashed waters.

The lea of Homa Mountain forms the southern shore of Kendu Bay, a charming little port village. Offshore small tugs tow barges along the coastline, their stacks sending pillars of black smoke skywards into the still air that heralds the sudden onset of a lake squall. Just two kilometres from the town is an unusual crater lake, Simbi, its emerald waters a sea of algae. There's also an enormous pelican breeding ground near here.

From Kendu Bay it's a short and pleasant cruise across the wide span of the Kavirondo to Kisumu, the waters alive with the lateen sails of the Luo fishing fleets. Their sturdy gaily-decorated canoes and sailing vessels are a picturesque part of Lake Victoria life, hand-crafted out of mahogany by the boat builders of the Suba tribe. These dhow-like boats are improvisations of the vessels introduced into these waters in the nineteenth-century by Arab traders from the coast. Today some are driven by powerful outboard motors, but it has done nothing to diminish Luo skills as watermen. One of the most colourful sights on these shores

are the annual regattas the villagers hold: the muscular oarsmen paddling their high-prowed canoes through the waters, skins gleaming with spray, waves creaming back from the bows, a study of graceful but powerful symmetry.

More than three million strong, the Luo range the shores of Victoria from Homa Bay in the south to Sio Port on the Uganda border in the north. Inland they extend well up the Nyando Escarpment and all along the fertile plains of Western and Nyanza provinces. Many have migrated in recent times to fish, farm or teach in every region of the country. The Luo claim they are like the water, with which they have such a close affinity — flowing everywhere until they find their own level.

Formerly a cattle-herding culture, they adopted fishing when they migrated south from Sudan several centuries ago. As well as fishing, they tend smallholdings, raising subsistence and cash crops, particularly sugar, and maintain herds of plump rich-yielding dairy cattle. But first and foremost they are fisherfolk and exploit all Kenya's freshwater lakes — even Lake Chala, the diamond on the bosom of Kilimanjaro, Lake Jipe and the Indian Ocean — including alkaline Turkana in the far north. They use a cunning maze trap at the mouths of the rivers which feed Victoria. The bewildered fish swim in easily enough but can find no way out.

The central town of Luoland is Kisumu, where Preston triumphantly invited his wife to hammer down the last rail of his five-and-a-half-year engineering odyssey to the great lake on 20 December 1901. The railhead was named Port Florence — not after Florence Preston but Florence Whitehouse, wife of the General Manager and Chief Engineer, who had visited the port earlier.

Now the work was done. The Lunatic Line was finished. But it was not until 1903 — the time it took to complete the many viaducts on the Mau Summit — that the first train pulled up in the new station. The cynics rejoiced, but not for long. It was this massive engineering work that acted as a catalyst to meld Kenya's more than forty different ethnic groups into a homogenous whole and ultimately inspire the birth of a nation. From this enterprise sprang the great farming industries of Kenya and a pattern of development, growth and trade that brought prosperity and opportunity to millions.

With a population approaching half a million, Kenya's third largest town is testament to the dynamic vigour of this still young nation, yet it retains a remarkably relaxed ambience in the shadows of the warehouses and industrial plants which have grown up since Independence. In recent years, the collapse of the East African Community has slowed down Kisumu's economic growth, for it was as East Africa's major lake port that it flourished with customs and immigration sheds alongside the warehouses.

The rail terminus is on the jetty where, until 1977, engines and wagons would be loaded on to the large, fast-moving rail ferries that criss-crossed and circumnavigated Lake Victoria's vast surface, carrying goods to Uganda and Tanzania. Tall white buildings dominate the town, which swelters in the twenty-four-hour humidity — more characteristic of central Africa than of Kenya's cool and breezy highlands. The enervating heat dictates Kisumu's easygoing way of life, but when Kenya's Division One soccer aces, Gor Mahia, meet in a league clash, there's no shortage

of energy either among the players of the fans. The club takes its name from one of the community's mythical heroes of long ago. More relaxed sport includes the Kisumu Yacht Club and the Golf Club where hippos along the fairways are a recognized hazard.

Thirty years after Preston's arrival, the line began to wind out of town again — across the Equator at Maseno — covering another sixty-five kilometres to the busy market town of Butere. West of this lie the malarial flatlands and swamps of Siaya District of Nyanza Province, covered only with small villages linked by a few minor roads.

From one of these towns, on the southern flanks of the large Yala Swamp, you climb a nearby hill revered in Luo history as the place where the first Luos arrived to settle after their long trek southwards. No wonder they stayed. The lush heat enfolds the body as you gaze upon the island-studded lake and the lagoon below. When these first settlers arrived 500 years ago, they clashed with the existing tenants, a Bantu group which they eventually ousted.

On the northern flanks of Yala is Sio, once called Port Victoria. It was perhaps a fancy of the early rail planners that the line would one day reach there, but it never did and Sio Port — just a small desultory village — serves principally as a ferry point to carry lakelanders into Uganda by boat or dugout canoe.

East of Butere stands the Nandi Escarpment, its southern extremity marked by the gentle folds of the Nandi Hills. The capital of this verdant land of flame trees and tea is the rustic town of Kapsabet, set at a cool and refreshing 6,400 feet. Traditionally pastoralists, the Nandi's skills at cattle

Above: Traders from Kendu Bay, following a centuries-old tradition, haul cattle salt by donkey train into the fertile Kisii highlands to barter for fruit and vegetables.

husbandry are self-evident: the Nandi herds produce more milk than any other district in the country. What could be more perfect? Here are tea and milk in abundance and just a few kilometres away, on the Chemelil-Mumias plains below, grows Kenya's sugar cane, yielding in one recent year a record 300,000 tons. No wonder this western sugarbowl is known as the land of milk and honey.

The contrasts between the two landscapes, separated only by the height of the escarpments, are as sharp and well-defined as the distinctive flavour of Nandi tea. All is quiet and peaceful in this rural wonderland. It's hard to believe that the Nandi were as fearsome and dedicated as the Maasai. From around 1895 to 1905, Nandi *esprit de corps* and military strategy earned them a martial reputation, surpassed only by the Zulu of South Africa and the Maasai. No raiders swarmed down to attack the railway builders as they carved their way to Butere in 1932, but little more than three decades earlier these lithe warriors tormented Preston and his railhead gangs.

They frequently trailed down from the hills to pillage the iron tracks for forging weapons and telegraph wires for crafting copper bracelets. The dry, scholarly Sir Charles Eliot displayed rare understanding of the thefts: 'One can imagine what thefts would be committed on a European railway if the telegraph wires were pearl necklaces and the rails first-rate sporting guns, and it is not surprising the Nandi yielded to the temptation.'

Not only did the Lunatic Line threaten their forest-clad heights, the coolies raped and sodomized their young women and boys. The Nandi were quick to exact retribution. The Nandi Rebellion, which took place at the end of November 1900, led to a fatal confrontation five years later with the overwhelming might of British forces — yet another sad stain on Britain's imperial history in Kenya.

In 1905 the British exacted sordid vengeance. The Nandi, who had earlier seized the prefabricated sections of the first boat to sail the lake, the *William Mackinnon*, thus delaying its launch by many months, were massacred in their hundreds, like the Gusii. During the expedition into their hilltop fortress, British forces killed one in every ten warriors, razed villages and seized the Nandi cattle. Their chief seer, Koitalel, similar to the Maasai *laibon*, negotiated a temporary truce, but when he went to meet the British for a long-term pow-wow on permanent peace, he was treacherously murdered in one of the most shameful incidents in colonial history.

The Nandi share a similar genesis myth in their oral history to that of the Maasai — culminating in a long migration which began when the great waters were divided by a tribal prophet. Though believing, like nearly all Kenya peoples, in one God, the Creator — known as Asis, the Supreme Being — the Nandi believe in liberal libations of milk, beer and offerings of food to pacify the ancestral spirits. They spit to ward off bad luck and, as the Kikuyu do, in a form of blessing also. Spittle sprayed on the chest and palms is potent blessing — the epitome of honest dealing and elegant courtesy.

Nandi distance runners have earned international renown in Olympic arenas as the world's finest: in one brief spell, Henry Rono accumulated an unprecedented four world records.

Rich in folklore, the tribe is renowned for its endless stock of riddles and proverbs. And way back in their history one of their great story-tellers introduced a rather large shaggy-dog tale that still features in the yarns told around the evening cooking fires. Like the Tibetan Abominable Snowman, *Yeti*, which roams the Himalaya, the Nandi Bear, *Chemoset*, has been resurrected by credulous western researchers and is said to roam the high forests. No matter how mythical, it's a story that every so often still makes a headline in the Kenya press.

The north-western slopes of the Nandi Hills are cloaked with a remarkable forest — unique in eastern Africa, but common on the other side of the continent. The Kakamega Forest is composed of trees indigenous to West Africa and as a result hosts rare and precious game and birdlife.

Kakamega town is the administrative centre of the Luhyia community, made up of seventeen sub-tribes, renowned for their love of music and, more recently, their passion for soccer. It echoes that of the voluble Merseysiders in north-west England and the Luhyia Club, AFC Leopards, carries the hopes and wishes of all these people in their endless quest for pan-African football trophies, rating alongside Gor Mahia as the nation's most accomplished team.

The trail Sergeant Ellis carved with Captain Sclater across Kenya's backbone in the 1890s from Fort Smith in Kikuyuland finally reached Kakamega in 1896. The town's other fame was as the seat of Kenya's Klondike Gold Rush in the 1930s, when more than a thousand prospectors staked their claim to what proved to be very sparse veins of the precious ore. Kenya was ever like that for most settlers — alluring and full of promises unfulfilled. Nonetheless you still find an occasional hardy local prospecting the Kakamega hillside's streams, panning for the proverbial alluvial treasure house and in Nairobi's streets you may meet some smooth-talking confidence trickster with promise that somewhere out there in the West is an El Dorado for the taking.

Above: Smiling Gusii child cradled on her sister's back.

The forest is Kakamega's real treasure, however: a remnant of the unbroken Equatorial jungle that, from west to east, as recently as four centuries ago arched across the continent; and its shadows are the haunt of species found nowhere else in Kenya, or in East Africa for that matter. Among them are some particularly venomous snakes, including the fat and sluggish Gabon viper and a high-living arboreal creature that is around only at night.

The pottos, a tiny bear-like animal without a tail — or, at least, only a rudimentary stump — has a rounded head, small ears and unequal limbs, and is known in many an African vernacular as 'half-a-tail'. Pottos live exclusively in the top storeys of their forest home — rarely, if ever, coming down to earth. It would indeed be difficult for it to do so. The movements of these cuddly-looking, slow motion 'teddy bear' creatures — usually seen frozen in the light of a flashlight glare — are as close to active inertia as the law of physics and description allow. Possibly, only the South American sloth is slower.

The forest is also home to one of the most fascinating of all Kenya's animals — the scaly-tailed flying squirrel. It belongs to a peculiar group of rodents, the *Anomalurus*, now extinct outside Africa. Though it does
162 not fly in the sense of a bird, it glides enormous distances with the help

of its cape, a flap of furred skin from wrist to ankle down the body and from ankle to tail. Spread out, this gliding membrane forms a very broad wind surface, enabling it to 'plane' long distances. In this fashion it can 'fly' as far as ninety metres.

Besides these two rarities, the forest — which is interspersed with open glades and grasslands — hosts abundant monkeys, small antelopes, and a wealth of bird life, including species normally endemic to West Africa. These include Kenya's only resident parrot population and the great blue turaco, a large and shiny bird, with its plumage all plumped up, the size of a turkey.

From Kakamega the road climbs up to Broderick Falls to rejoin the 1920s spur of the Uganda Railway, which finally linked the two countries. Until the 1970s, nothing much distinguished this place except the 170-foot deep cascading waterfalls — named after an early European visitor to this region — in the thick forests which cloaked the region.

A few kilometres above the falls, on the escarpment, stands Chetambe's Fort, scene of an 1895 massacre by a British punitive expedition against the Bukusu tribe of the Luhyia. The warriors, dug in behind a 100-metre-long moat-like rampart, fell like flies before the spluttering fire of the British expedition's Maxim machine gun — with only shields for defence and spears for weapons.

Then in the 1970s, in a Ken-Indo partnership organized by the World Bank, the place was chosen as the site of Kenya's paper milling industry. The falls provided an ideal source of water close to one of Kenya's great logging regions. Today more than 20,000 people depend on this industry for their livelihood in the town that's built of paper. Bustling Webuye continues to grow fast as demand for paper in education-hungry Kenya soars.

The railway descends quickly through the boulder-studded hills, open grasslands, smallholdings and sugar fields, through Bungoma — a prosperous but dull administrative town — to Malaba, where it enters Uganda.

Southwards from Broderick Falls, however, you can follow the course of the track up to the high Uasin Gishu plateau to Leseru — another town famous for its cheeses — where in 1926, another branch line was built, stretching across the fertile grasslands of the Trans-Nzoia plateau to Kitale on the slopes of Mount Elgon, which straddles the Uganda border.

As the track cut through Soy, Elgon's great, free-standing mass dominated the horizon. Noted for its country club, Soy's remnant herd of the rare Rothschild's giraffe became famous in 1974 when Jock and Betty Leslie Melville chose a six-month-old female, Daisy Rothschild, to move to their home in Nairobi's Karen suburb.

There's an irrepressible feel of the English countryside about the meadowlands around Kitale, which stands 6,200 feet above sea level. With avenues of giant blue gums lining either side of the road, this rustic farm and market centre has undeniable charm: Kitale Station is a reflection of the graceful days of the leisurely steam travel which inspired it. Now noted for its fruit orchards, and as headquarters of the giant Kenya Seed Company, Kitale's bracing air and relaxed life styles, far from the tensions and milieu of metropolitan living, encourage longevity.

Benign Kitale became a boom town briefly during the 1970s coffee bonanza. Ugandan coffee was smuggled across the border on the back road that cuts high over the shoulders of Mount Elgon, the magnificent backdrop against which the town stands. It was an old slaving station at this place on the main caravan route between Uganda and Bagamoyo in Tanzania. A circle of stones in the car park of the timbered Kitale Club once surrounded the ring to which the slaves were chained. A century or more later, Kitale's business men and farmers meet in the bar and at weekends drive the long, lush fairways of the club's challenging golf course. Whatever your handicap, the looming mass of Mount Elgon beyond the greens is inspiration enough to essay a round.

Unequalled for its perspectives and sense of solitude, 14,178-foot-high Mount Elgon is a mountaineer's mountain, even though it offers no serious climbing challenges. This is one of the loveliest and most unspoilt of all Kenya's national parks. Indeed, if you are fit and hardy enough to labour up the elephant trails through its glorious forests, you can walk its moorland heights for days without meeting another soul. Should you chance to do so, the odds are that it will be a mountain enthusiast from far away — America, Europe or Australia — lured across the seas by the wealth of mountain lore that Elgon inspires in all who explore the crater of this long extinct volcano and tramp the surrounding heady heaths of tussock grass and wild flora, including lobelia and giant groundsel. Burgeoning under the unique combination of high, rarefied air,

164 unfiltered ultraviolet rays and freezing nights, these specimens flourish

Above: Iteso pottery echoes tribal traditions, shaping the large urns used for communal drinking. Filled with millet beer, the pot is placed in the centre of a group which draws the beer from it through two-metre-long straws.

better here than on Mount Kenya or Kilimanjaro, a delight to the botanist.

Though lower in altitude, Elgon's massive base is far larger than either of the two higher mountains. It was known to the Maasai, whose herds once grazed the Trans-Nzoia — a remnant group, the il-Kony, still live high up on the mountain — as Ol Doinyo Igoon, the Mountain of the Breast. The lower slopes of the mountain are pitted with caves long used by the il-Kony as night corrals for their cattle. One of these, Kitum Cave, was the inspiration for Rider Haggard's adventure drama, *She*. It's also been the inspiration for a television documentary about the phenomenon of Elgon's elephants which 'mine' salt in the cave, gouging it out during the night from the walls deep inside the mountain, sometimes precipitating a roof fall that traps one or two of these great pachyderms.

Ancient beyond comprehension, Elgon feels like a link with the beginning of time. Founded in 1949, the 169-square-kilometre National Park embraces the topmost heights on the Kenya side of the border with Uganda — which cuts right across the rim and through the centre of the crater. Indeed, Wagagai, the highest peak, is on the Uganda side of the crater rim, but the variation between one side of the crater and the other is minimal. Sudek, on the Kenya side, rises to 14,140 feet, just thirty-six feet lower. Favourite for many, however, is 13,880-foot-high Koitobos peak.

Three gates lead into the park and through the bamboo forest into the giant stands of ancient podocarpus to the moorlands — the most popular

Opposite: Figurine shaped and fired by Iteso potters.

165

Left: Renowned hippo hunters, the 75,000-strong Suba community on the shores of Lake Victoria celebrated each kill in song and dance. Now that hippo hunting is forbidden, the Suba menfolk concentrate on fishing, leaving the drying and sale of their catch to their womenfolk.

being the Chorlim Gate off the Endebess road, which is reached along the dirt road that cuts through the rich farmlands below the forest. There's a little-used luxury lodge near the gate which flourished briefly during the 1970s as an overnight hostelry for the coffee barons. Fittingly, too, for if nothing else, Mount Elgon Lodge is the epitome of the European stately home with its baronial dining room, public rooms and superb gardens. It was built by an aristocratic English settler as a nostalgic evocation of his ancestral seat.

He chose one of the finest panoramic landscapes in the world. From the gardens the guests gaze out down the southern slopes and across the tranquil meadows and fields of the Trans-Nzoia to the distant blue-grey outline of the Cheranganis. Above the manor, however, the view is near vertical as Elgon's forests climb towards the sky.

Different species of game lurk beneath the centuries-old trees that rise 100 feet or more — clean, straight-stemmed, crowned with evergreen foliage — to the sunlight they crave. In the glades and dappled undergrowth beneath, the ever-alert, always nervous buck, duiker, and minnows pause frozen in the panic of discovery as great herds of buffalo forage for fodder. Within the forests are well-marked trails. On either side lies evidence of Elgon's impatient elephants — the lifeless boles of the giant podos broken like tumbleweed, pushed aside, folded over and snapped by these animal foresters which, like man, are heedless of their own environment. Nature's trails are less spacious than mankind's. The thick tangle of ancient trees and new-born saplings seems to bar the way. But the limbs torn down by the elephant hide the tracks over which these seemingly lumbering giants deftly tip-toe their way up and down mountain ridges that rise and fall a thousand feet in half a kilometre.

Nature is the calendar — the precise week, month, year, even the century, seem unimportant. All phases of forest life are part of nature's eternal cycle. When life becomes too ancient, it dies and falls to the forest floor to begin the cycle anew. Daily, the fetid compost rotting at the feet of Elgon's giant trees sustains and renews their life. In the dark shadows of a thicket, giant butterflies flit from leaf to leaf and shadows move; perhaps a leopard, or possibly just wishful fancy. The stillness is hypnotic and enchanting. Insects whirr and buzz among the wild flowers and weeds. The shadows move fitfully in the sluggish stir of a fading breeze. Trees and shrubs rustle in its passage. The silence has a thousand eloquent tongues to seduce the listener.

At night, after the moon slips over the topmost peak, the barking of the baboons in the forest and the sawing cough of the leopard tell of an unseen drama. The morning search reveals the carcass of a young buffalo no more than 100 metres from the camp.

When railways were the fashion, it was once fancied a line might run from the Cape to Cairo. But Kitale is the end of the line. East lies the daunting barrier of the dramatic Cherangani Hills, Kenya's only range of fold mountains, hiding within their forests some of the finest mountain landscapes in the world. The 11,000-foot-high range forms the northern end of the Elgeyo Marakwet Escarpment, falling more than 8,000 feet in places to the baking floor of the Kerio Valley, gateway to the deserts of Kenya's north far below.

Within the folds of its hills, the Cherangani embraces a place sacred to Kenya nationalists — the little town of Kapenguria where, in the 1950s, the colonial government staged a rigged show trial of Mzee Jomo Kenyatta and six other leaders of the independence struggle. After a shower of perjured and fabricated evidence, they were sentenced to a savage nine-year incarceration far away on the burning shores of Lake Turkana. Now the schoolroom in Kapenguria, where the trial was staged, is a national shrine to the memory of the nation's founding father.

In the tranquility of this sylvan setting, which reflects an atmosphere of peace, the sentence seems all the more savage. Clothed with stately forests and bamboo groves, the Cheranganis are a natural wonderland of trout streams, endless vistas and rare game like the bongo, the shy night-time antelope found elsewhere in Kenya only on the Aberdares. Nothing

in the world emulates the run of the bongo. It goes into a crouching position and throws its head well back, the horns lying flat along its back. In the thick tangle of thicket, trees and bamboo in which it lives, this allows it to move swiftly through the undergrowth. This elusive creature — with twelve to fourteen vertical white stripes down its flanks — is the largest of Kenya's forest antelopes.

One of its closest kin is the sitatunga which in Kenya is found only within a small Cherangani swamp, now preserved as Saiwa National Park, perhaps the smallest national park in the world. This postage-stamp sized sanctuary — close to Kapenguria — covers just over two square kilometres. Vehicles are not allowed, and Saiwa's rare visitors make their way through the jungle and swamp on foot. The main trail is a wooden walkway above the reeds and along a jungle path where black and white colobus monkeys flit through the trees, vervets scamper across the ground and you may catch a glimpse of the immensely wise, mandarin-like face of the de Brazza monkey. In the canopy of trees, rare birds flit from perch to perch, including turacos, hornbills, and kingfishers.

Viewing platforms are raised above the waters of the swamp, where visitors watch in silence for their first sight of the sitatunga. It's a remarkable example of nature's virtuosity. It has evolved so that its two-toed, elongated hooves spread out widely to dissipate its weight, enabling it to move about on mats of floating weeds — thus giving it the appearance of walking on water. But sitatunga are truly amphibious. Alarmed, they sink into the water, only the tips of their nostrils showing. They are also known as marshbuck and swim adeptly.

From Kapenguria, a new trans-African highway to Sudan drops precipitously in a series of twisting hairpin bends and esses to the desert floor. Ahead lies one of the most rugged landscapes in the world, sere and burnt out, covering at least one-third of Kenya. The highland plateaux which overlook this haunting but magical region of Kenya were as far as the railway builders dared to venture.

7· Cradle of Mankind

There are three springboards into Kenya's far north. Take the railway to Nanyuki on the shoulders of Mount Kenya, to Thomson's Falls, or disembark at Kitale Station. Whichever you choose, you will soon arrive at the lip of the escarpment, formed aeons ago, which gazes down on a dustbowl that, more than anywhere else, is considered to be the one place on earth where mankind was born. From any railhead, nothing prepares the first-time visitor for the sudden transition from mountain greenery to blazing desert. Within minutes the cool air is left behind and shirts and blouses cling to the body.

The perspectives and dimensions for a first-time witness of these panoramic landscapes give pause for thought. There's an elemental mysticism about Kenya which eventually envelops almost everybody who roams its immense horizons with their distant escarpments and blue-grey mountains, where looming storm clouds sometimes darken the sky.

In Kenya's still remote regions, where great herds of wildlife move slowly among the golden grasslands, the feeling arises that this must have been Eden. Everything seems almost too perfect. But the herds that moved across Kenya's great desert lands a century ago have diminished. One hundred years of drought and wind have increased the erosion. The sun has blistered and scorched once fertile soils.

Yet if any place on earth has rightful claim to be the Cradle of Mankind it is the badlands of northern Kenya. Lance Morrow, in his 1987 *Time* magazine essay, 'Africa', wrote of the 'shadowless clarity of creation' he experienced and of Kenya's 'smiting Equatorial light'. Its brilliance is sometimes overwhelming. Morrow, clearly smitten by all things Kenyan — the harsh reality of ritual life and death in the bush, the extraordinary rhythm of mortality — concluded that it was a 'last glimpse of that shadowless life previous to time and thought . . . a pure connection to the imagination of God'.

For many, including the scientists who probe and sift the fossil beds of Koobi Fora on the shores of Lake Turkana, this is indeed the Land of Genesis. But the lush imagery of Eden is nowhere in evidence. This paucity of resources and lack of material profit provides an antithesis to today's world of technology and mushrooming living standards, and preserves life styles which serve as the richest living reminder of what mankind sprang from and was.

The new road from Kitale winds down to this Cradle of Mankind through the Cheranganis into the Kerio Valley, a secondary rift with sheer walls, where the seasonal Turkwel River, spawned in the forested slopes of 10,500-foot-high Mount Sondang, thunders over a dramatic gorge. A French-sponsored hydro-power project is changing the face of the Turkwel where it leaves these high cliffs — building a dam to tap its waters for the energy so vital to Kenya.

The valley floor and the cliff faces are the haunt of the Marakwet who have long utilized the waters, centuries ago building a series of aqueducts, canals and viaducts — to a high degree of sophisticated design — which channel the waters along the precipitous ledges and over ravines to irrigate the verdant little farms they cultivate. Ownership of these canals and ducts goes way back in time and the whole community now maintains and repairs them. But ancient ways are still practised.

172

Above: Turkana elder in tribal finery. Warriors of this 250,000-strong community of pastoral nomads are famed for their desert bushcraft, survival techniques and ferocious fighting.

Preceding pages: Perched on a desolate lava hill, a Turkana warrior gazes out over the scorching floor of Suguta Valley, one of the hottest places on earth.

Above: Colourful parade of Pokot youngsters in circumcision group lines up for initiation. The ceremony is spaced at intervals ranging from between ten to fifteen years, but not all Pokot practise circumcision.

Courtship of a Marakwet woman takes place after her circumcision and is a stylish, graceful affair. The suitor visits her home to discuss marriage with the girl's parents, but only after he has been given the go ahead by the girl. She acknowledges this by handing him the stick she was given to mark her intiation into womanhood. In return, he must hand over his spear and other weapons. When this is done, he can begin the dowry negotiations. For all this, the couple still have to be particularly lucky to be matched: there are many taboos — clan, totem group and so forth — which may prove a barrier.

The desert floor beneath — all the way to the Karapokot escarpment on the Uganda border — is occupied by the Pokot, the Marakwet's once-belligerent neighbours, who range up to the edge of the Turkana lands. These badlands inspire hardy and proud independence and a tradition of warriorhood. The land yields little or nothing. The soil is worn out. The people are hardy, spartan and indifferent to the materialism which has assailed the rest of the world. In their natural pride they despise greed. The only profit is survival: simply staying alive is indicative of a wealth of human resourcefulness.

Black, brown and grey volcanic monuments burst through the desert floor, creating a tangled and serrated landscape. Pastures are rare, water

Above: Samburu mother shaves son's head as he prepares for circumcision and the transition from boyhood to manhood.

even more so, and cattle are prized. The Pokot, traditionally rustlers, share with the Turkana a love of fierce and fiendish fighting weapons: hooked finger knives, wrist knives, hand knives with sheaths, spears, the mandatory bow — arrows tipped with a lethal poison — and leather shield combine to form a formidable arsenal of hand-to-hand combat weapons.

The Turkwel flows along the base of their north-western escarpment before veering east at Lodwar, dusty desert capital of the vast Turkana region. By the time it reaches the Jade Sea, it is sapped of all vigour, sometimes run dry for months on end. The new trans-African highway has brought these remote regions into close contact with the mainstream of modern Kenyan society. Lodwar, where Mzee Jomo Kenyatta spent the final two years of his incarceration in a small bungalow, is developing swiftly. But only the cattle trails of the Turkana pastoralists and warriors carve through this sere landscape.

The only growing things are thorn bushes, their roots radiating as far as twenty metres in search of moisture, an occasional baobab, some heat and dust loving succulents and desert grass. To the Turkana's 250,000-strong society, this is cherished land. For centuries they attacked their neighbours — and more recently the British — to keep what they have of it and to take more. British presence in Turkana was established in 1905, when the Baringo District Commissioner led a foot expedition along the length of the Kerio river from its source on 9,000-foot-high Kapkut Mountain, near Timboroa on the Equator, to its mouth on the lake's south-western shores.

Above: Groomed by her relatives, dressed in finery, a Samburu bride prepares for marriage after undergoing circumcision in accordance with tribal tradition.

Turkana qualities are not just heroic. As a people they mellow with long acquaintance. They have a remarkable language: it includes twenty-three verbs simply to describe a person's walk, making them highly articulate by any measure. Some have turned to fishing in the Jade Sea as a way of livelihood — without too much enthusiasm. Like the Maasai, they count cattle as all things to all men. The more the better. The Turkana range all the way along Lake Turkana's western shores as far as the Ilemi Triangle through little known places marked perhaps by nothing more than a police post.

One of these, called Lokitaung, however, became known the world over in the 1950s, when Kenyatta spent seven years in this harsh inhospitable climate, in a vain bid by the British to frustrate Kenya's nationalist ambitions. But Mzee Jomo Kenyatta and his colleagues survived their ordeal to lead Kenya into the family of free nations.

Not far from Lokitaung, however, a curious legacy of British imperial rule survives. At the far north-west corner of the lake the borders of Sudan, Ethiopia, and Kenya, merge in the Ilemi Triangle. By some unwritten pact Kenya has inherited this ancient writ of colonial administration — and thus it is Kenya's police forces which patrol this no-man's land between three nations.

From the railhead at Nyahururu a new tarmac road sweeps down through the Marmanet Forest to dusty Rumuruti, southernmost border of Samburu land and a cattle town where once European settlers, raising their beef herds in the arid savannah around these parts, met and quaffed ales in the town's old club. Most have now gone, and beyond

175

Left: Standing on its hind legs, the gerenuk spends a great deal of its life searching for the lusher leaves found high on the acacia thorns and other desert shrubs. Their name derives from the Somali language, meaning 'giraffe-necked'.

Above: Reticulated giraffe. Reaching heights of up to eighteen feet when the world's tallest creature lowers its head to drink it maintains a stable blood pressure through a series of complex valves and blood reservoirs in the neck.

Rumuruti the road becomes a gravel track on its way to Lake Turkana.

The southernmost boundary of Samburu territory lies just beyond Rumuruti and is bounded in the north by Mount Kulal on the eastern shores of Lake Turkana. This 30,000-square-kilometre wedge-shaped triangle is where the 75,000-strong tribe — a splinter group of Maasai whose name in the Maa language means 'butterfly' — settled some centuries ago, while the rest continued their southward advance. At the centre is 8,200-foot-high Poro Mountain, which rises above the Samburu administrative centre of Maralal. Rich in its game life, zebra, buffalo, eland and leopard, Poro is a magnificent backdrop for the tin-roofed, one-street 'capital' where the Samburu stand heron-like on one leg, spear in hand, at every corner. There's a pleasant lodge with roaring log fires at night where through the picture window, you can watch the wildlife that congregates on the lawns.

From Maralal you drive through some of the toughest terrain in the world — South Horr, overlooking the dusty bowl of Lake Suguta, one of the hottest places on earth — and down rocky, boulder-strewn trails to Loiyangalani — 'place of the trees' — home of the el Molo people. It was the way Teleki and von Hohnel travelled on their journey of discovery to the lake, which they christened Rudolf, after one of their Austrian princes.

The el Molo were once incorrectly described as the smallest tribe in the world. Not a tribe certainly, but a group of dropouts and drifters and Ndorobos from other communities who have formed their own cultural identity, renowned as hippo and crocodile hunters. Living the most meagre of existences, they were malnourished and crippled by rickets

Above: Female greater kudu. The males are distinguished by horns that are among the most magnificent in the antelope kingdom.

Right: Seen from the side, it is easy to imagine the oryx as the mythical unicorn. In profile the splendid horns merge as one to match exactly the images drawn so long ago. Beisa oryx can go long periods without water.

Above: Aboard a fragile doum-palm raft, two el-Molo youngsters fish the jade waters of 6,400-square-kilometre Lake Turkana with harpoon.

and other calcium-deficient diseases from drinking the Lake's alkaline waters. Today the group, numbering fewer than a thousand people, is taking advantage of the education and health schemes modern Kenya offers and, aided by dedicated missionaries, is gradually being brought into the mainstream of society. Nonetheless, their traditions remain a living link with mankind's own beginnings, which may have not been too far north of their sheltered bays on the lake's south-eastern shores.

The first Europeans to stumble across the sight of Turkana's waters just a century ago were the Austrian adventurers Count Samuel Teleki and von Hohnel. Alkaline and barely drinkable, Turkana's 6,400-square-kilometre surface is capricious. Sometimes it is calm and unruffled, often it is turbulent with an impression of malevolence.

Three islands — prosaically named South, Central and North — mark the 290-kilometre length of Turkana, at its broadest at the bulging waist of Ferguson's Gulf, where it measures fifty-six kilometres. These islands were raised by volcanic eruptions. Barren Central Island off Ferguson's Gulf is still steaming. Camping on the beach — once the main breeding ground for Turkana's Nile crocodiles — is memorable. At night, whiffs of smoke erupt from the largest of its three craters as a full moon rises swiftly behind its bulking silhouette — bright enough to read a book by!

The largest island, South Island, is associated with a human tragedy involving Sir Vivien Fuchs, who led an expedition to its shores in 1934. Three days after landing, he returned to the mainland, sending Dr S. W.

Dyson to join W. H. R. Martin on 28 July 1934. Fuchs gave them explicit

Right: Fearless hunters of hippo and crocodiles, an el-Molo mother prepares a young crocodile for the family breakfast.

orders to return to the mainland by 13 August. They were never seen again.

North Island is infested with venomous snakes which have drifted down from the Omo delta on rafts of papyrus. Turkana and its shores host some of the world's most poisonous reptiles. To the saw-scaled vipers and night adders, puff adders and cobras also add lethal scorpions.

Few sizeable ships have ever sailed Turkana's waters, and of those that have, many foundered. The vessels which now ply the lake number about 500 fishing craft and the eight-ton Scottish-built trawler, *Halcyon*, belonging to the Fisheries Department.

Turkana is rich in its bounty. Yields of forty tons — more than forty fish species flourish in the lake — have been recorded. For millions of years the lake's crocodile population have lived in perfect balance with their environment, feeding voraciously on the giants and minnows of the deep. Nile perch weigh up to 400 kilograms and there are tilapia, tiger fish and many more lurking beneath Turkana's often stormy surface.

This natural order has maintained a stable crocodile population estimated at around 12,000 creatures, the last great colony of crocodiles in the world. These saurians reach lengths of five metres and their biology has remained unchanged for at least 130 million years.

The lake offers the same hospitality to a rich variety of bird life: more than 350 species of resident and migratory birds depend on the Jade Sea's rich lacustrine life. Over the years the spectacle has attracted many ornithologists, including Prince Philip, the Duke of Edinburgh, and his son, Prince Charles.

Turkana draws its strength from the Omo, Ethiopia's second largest river, which begins its 965-kilometre journey south on 9,500-foot-high Mount Amara west of Addis Ababa, the Ethiopian capital. When it

179

reaches Turkana, swollen by floods and many tributaries, it cuts a thirty-kilometre-wide swathe through an impenetrable thicket of swamp and papyrus to discharge twenty million cubic metres of life-sustaining water each year into East Africa's fourth largest lake.

The sun sucks it out again. Under such intense evaporation, Lake Turkana shrank dramatically during the first half of this century. In 1902 Sanderson's Gulf on the north-western shores was fifty kilometres long and sixteen kilometres wide. connected to the main lake by a sound five kilometres across. Now it is dry land. Many thousands of years ago, when the lake was 150 metres deeper it was connected to the White Nile Basin by an outlet through the Lotikipi Plain beyond Lokitaung, where it cut a deep gorge. The centuries have eroded this ravine to expose fossil forests.

From the third railhead at Nanyuki the descent from crisp mountain air, wheatfields and verdant smallholdings to the savage sting of the sun and the brown baked semi-desert is swift and dramatic. The smooth modern road plunges from Timau's rarefied heights close to 10,000 feet, on the shoulders of Mount Kenya, down more than 7,000 feet in fewer than forty kilometres.

Suddenly, beyond the Islamic mosque on the outskirts of Isiolo, the glittering tin roofs close in on either side. For all its squat, nondescript, simple single-storey main street — like something out of the Wild West — Isiolo is gateway, if not capital, to a good third of Kenya.

It's at the checkpoint on the northern boundary of the town, where the tarmac peters out into the Great North Highway, a sea of corrugations

Above: Somali herdboy waters his camels. Hardy, independent and proud, Kenya's 450,000-strong Somali community roam a vast area of the northern deserts, herding their camels and cattle in a hostile, arid environment.

Above: Gabbra family carry their homesteads across the wastes of the Dida Galgala, the 'Plains of Darkness', in northern Kenya. These collapsible homes aboard their camel caravans conjure up true pictures of the ships of the desert. With fewer than 50,000 people, the Gabbra are survivors of successive epochs of war and disaster which have taken place during the last 150 years.

that heads to Addis Ababa, the Ethiopian capital, or the eastward dirt road into the trackless wastes of this desert, that the traveller records his departure.

East, vast and still largely unexplored, lies a truly great wilderness. Once patrolled by scouts on camelback, it was the scene of a bitter guerilla war between Somali bandits and nationalists during the 1960s, who claimed this land as Somalia's. After Kenya's Independence it was closed to visitors and the general public for many years. But work on vital projects — oil exploration and water drilling — continued.

Most of the people who roam this region are hardy nomads, ethnic Kenya Somali and the Gabbra. It's a land to numb the mind. Hardly a blade of grass peeps through the unproductive soil. The earth is bleached. The heat deadens the senses and the sun blinds. Mirages shimmer on the horizon. Water is rare, sometimes foul, but always precious. Nomad's Land is no-man's land except the Somali's and the Gabbra. No wonder the Gabbra call it Dida Galgalu. The nearest English translation means Plains of Darkness. If you walk anywhere in this area you will ask yourself how anything or anyone can survive. Yet the nomads live.

Culturally, the Gabbra are close to the Borana group, from which they derive their name. With their fine foreheads, skin oiled and glistening, many of these 30,000 people appear like patriarchs from an Old Testament lithograph. Their environment has produced a unique social structure forming a well-orchestrated, well co-ordinated, highly articulate pastoral community.

The Somali spread farther east — from Mandera close to the Ogaden where the Ethiopian and Somali borders meet — down through el Wak to Wajir, an administrative centre peopled only by settled desert folk and Kenya civil servants and officials. It retains a relic of the eccentricity which characterized Britain's colonial rule in these remote places. Three hundred kilometres from the nearest water, visitors are invited to enlist as members of the Royal Wajir Yacht Club, a prefix it earned from a member of Britain's Royal Family in pre-Independence days.

Featureless to all but those who roam its hidden trails, it's easy to get lost in Kenya's Northern Frontier District — NFD. Cling to the sandy trail between Wajir and Mado Gashi or you'll soon become hopelessly disorientated. The castellated walls of a desert fortress, like a prop from a Hollywood remake of the French Foreign Legion, mark Habaswein, but the defences are real — not fibreglass — for in this wild country bandits and outlaws still roam. It may explain why the next town on the road, Mado Gashi, is distinguished by the fact that within all this sprawling area only here — where the boundaries of Kenya's two largest provinces, the Rift Valley and North-Eastern, meet — do you find two police headquarters. Though you can travel thousands of kilometres almost anywhere else in this region without seeing a policeman, at Mado Gashi there are too many.

An expedition in these parts soon convinces you why there's a signing-in ceremony at the Isiolo checkpost. Not only eastward but for those travelling northward, too, including the visitor to the three game sanctuaries not too far from Isiolo: Samburu and Buffalo Springs National Reserves and Shaba National Reserve. Samburu is only fifty kilometres into the badlands, yet in time and place far removed from mainstream Kenya.

Battlements made of scarps and fallen boulders rise up out of the thorn scrub but where the stone and dirt road lurches down a dip and over a dried-up river, *wadi*, the rugged hills to the north-west vanish from view.

A gerenuk, startled as it stands on tip-toe to reach the remnants of last season's greenery, bounds away in a disconcerting zig-zag. The giraffe-necked gazelle was unknown to science until as recently as 1878. It spends a great deal of its life on its hind legs searching for the lusher leaves found high on the acacia thorn and other desert shrubs on which it thrives. Its name derives from the Somali language. As it has learned to use its rear legs to stand in a vertical posture while feeding, so its neck has evolved through the milleniums to become longer and longer. Antelopes of the desert, gerenuks survive without water, drawing all the liquid they need from their diet.

These elegant creatures run in a fascinating manner. Extremely swift, they bring their long necks down in line with their slender backs and suddenly — because of the extreme length of their stride — appear about half their normal size.

In the distance, short tails wagging incessantly, a neurotic herd of gazelle crop the grass and beyond them, through a blaze of perennial olive green riverine thorn, a line of swaying elephant ambles slowly forward.

Covering an area of 104 square kilometres, Samburu is one of the few sanctuaries in Kenya which is home to the Grevy's zebra, notably

Opposite: Pastoral nomads renowned as warriors, in recent years some of the Turkana have turned to fishing. Nile perch and other species caught in Lake Turkana are sun-dried on the shores of Ferguson's Gulf.

different from the Burchells — or common — zebra, and to the rarer Beisa oryx and the blue-shanked Somali ostrich. The neighbouring Buffalo Springs Reserve actually abuts Samburu with no noticeable change in species or topography, giving visitors a wide terrain to cover during their stay.

The reserve's central feature is the broad swathe of the Ewaso Ngiro which upstream plummets over Thomson's Falls. In spate its waters quickly swell and become a raging torrent. Early in 1986, it dried up during a prolonged drought which came to an abrupt end when a flash flood three metres deep rolled down its dry bed — a wall of water sweeping away all before it. Unlike most rivers, these waters never reach the sea. They bury themselves in the Lorien Swamp near the desert town of Habaswein in the east. On their way from Samburu, they flow through the nearby Shaba Game Reserve, less popular than the other two but beloved by the late Joy Adamson who made a camp here to continue her work on rehabilitating leopard to the wild. In 1980 she was brutally murdered in this remote spot.

The Great North Road divides Shaba from Buffalo Springs and Samburu, and then thrusts northward into a starkly dramatic wilderness of desert and mountain. From Archer's Post — named after an early English settler who made his camp here and which is now a military training ground — the Great North Road heads for the brooding sugarloaf profile of 6,500-foot-high Lololokwe.

Just before you reach the base of this gaunt rocky hump, a dirt road veers west through Wamba, a lively trading post overlooked by the 8,820-foot-high Warges Mountain, into Samburu country and the lush forest lands of the Lorogi Plateau in the Karisia Hills. It was from Wamba that writer John Hillaby began his *Journey to the Jade Sea* by camel caravan. Great mountain ranges — like the Nyiru Mountains on the south shores of Turkana and the Ol Doinyo Lenkiyo and Ndoto ranges in the east — make the Samburu's pastoral landscapes stunningly beautiful, though ever harsh.

Hillaby was overwhelmed by the panorama that unfolded when he reached the edge of one of the great plateaux. It was, he wrote, like 'looking over the edge of the world. The frontier plains stretched out towards Ethiopia, a boundless expanse of sand and lava dust, broken only by the wrecks of ancient volcanoes, some with exquisite breast-like cones, straight-sided and nippled with rosettes of magma; others had been worn down by the wind until, like the flat backs of a school of whales, they seemed to be swimming away, line astern, across a sea of sand.'

North-east lies the Ol Doinyo Lenkiyo Range, surmounted by the craggy 7,792-foot peak of Mount Matthews, named thus by Count Teleki, after Sir Lloyd Matthews, Commander-in-Chief of the Sultan of Zanzibar's Army, for the help the Austrian expedition was given. Martial eagles circle on the strong thermals hunting for prey in the sheer ravines below.

Beyond this range stands Kenya's least-known and least visited game sanctuary, the Losai National Reserve, in the mountains that rise up out of the Kaisut Desert. Virtually impenetrable by four-wheel drive vehicle, at the middle is the medical mission of Ngoronet with its airstrip. The only comfortable way in which to visit this 1,807-square-kilometre natural paradise is by light plane.

But, though beautiful to the visitor, existence in this region is life at its harshest. The missions tend to the needs of the Rendille camel pastoralist, close friends and distant kin of the Samburu. The Rendille's rocky wilderness covers around 20,000 square kilometres, much of it low altitude desert burning under the sun. Rainfall seldom exceeds seven inches a year. This terrain makes herding an arduous and sometimes dangerous task. Children are apprenticed in it from the time they walk until they reach puberty. Thereafter, now durable, courageous and unflinching, they are allowed out with the family camel herds on their own, often walking fearsome distances in search of water.

Kenya is exemplified by its tradition of hospitality. The peaceful stranger who attends an unknown village is welcomed with an openness that overwhelms. Paradoxically, the poorer the home, the poorer the person, the richer the welcome. Amongst the poorest in material posessions, the Rendille rank among the most generous of hosts — particularly to their own. Tradition makes a niggard of the Rendille who refuses the loan of a heifer camel to any of his tribe who ask it. It is an honour to oblige. There is prestige to be gained, but the result is ironic. Some of the richest stockholders in Rendille society walk about as virtual paupers — but with a claim or interest in almost every herd they see.

At Laisamis, where it enters the Kaisut, the Great North Road cuts through the lowland part of the reserve. Work on the road, built by Kenya's unique National Youth Service, was often delayed during the 1960s by marauding Somali *shifta* bandits. In the Kaisut, however, it was the virtually impassable terrain which bogged down work. Flash floods during the rare but torrential rains devastated road camps and bridge works. Incredible to believe in a desert such as this. Walls of raddled rock stand on either side of the road — rocks which look like disorderly dumps of abandoned and rusted cannon ball and shot. They can rip the bottom out of the car in seconds. Hiring a lorry to move the vehicle is often a long and costly process.

It was at this spot just before the First World War that the military martinet Colonel J. H. Patterson of the *Maneaters of Tsavo* fame disgraced his regiment's colours. His service commission ended, he had become a big game hunter. At the camp Patterson set up at Laisamis, one of his clients shot himself after finding his wife locked in the hero's arms in their tent.

At the foot of Marsabit Mountain is the mission village of Logologo, where the Milgis Lugga passes under one of the road bridges. One night a wall of water thirty metres deep roared down from the Ndoto Mountains along this dried-up river bed sweeping all — including the bridge and foundations — before it. In a wave of roaring disaster, the work of months was swept away in seconds.

Marsabit lies on the slopes of the mountain, a bleached brown monochrome of a town, where familiar petrol signs flap listlessly in the sluggish breeze and the rusted ghosts of yesteryear's safari form untidy piles of broken metals. The Great North Road is a backbreaker.

Capital of a sprawling administrative region, Marsabit is where many cultures meet — usually in the utilitarian bars where the atmosphere is

Above: Rendille women fashion an elegant braided coxcomb at the birth of their first-born son and only remove it — as a mark of mourning — when either the husband or the son dies.

185

warmer than the decor. Astonishingly in such an isolated part of the world, Marsabit boasts a microwave telephone link with the rest of the world.

Above: Rendille family leading camels through the Kaisut Desert between the Ndoto Mountains and Marsabit.

The town is as hot as the desert below: the grass brown, parched and patchy. But, only two kilometres away, the dirt track halts at the gate of 2,088-square-kilometre Marsabit National Reserve. Once through the gate and round the first bend, the forest closes in and you have entered another world wherein marvellous secrets of fish and fowl, beast and bird, are revealed in magic tree-lined craters. At least fifty-two species of eagle, hawk and falcon nest in the sheer 650- to 700-foot-high cliffs, amid stands of juniper and podo, which give the reserve's many craters a green fur lining. They are nourished by the unusual early morning mists which, with the reserve's elephants, make Marsabit a marvellous phenomenon.

Born out of volcanic fire, Marsabit is shaped by these mists. Each night the heat drawn from the desert cools, takes form and an hour or two before dawn clamps its clammy fingers around Marsabit's 4,600-foot-high peak, rarely releasing its grip before early afternoon. For centuries its cold and wet touch has quenched the thirst of the olive and the cedar and laid tendrils of Spanish moss across the branches to keep them cool when the afternoon sun glows warm. The bowls of the craters form natural amphitheatres. An elephant known as Mohamed, scion of Ahmed the Great, who was a living legend protected by Presidential decree, often leads his harem to the marsh grass at the rim of the Sokorte Guda bowl, perhaps one and a half kilometres in diameter. Marsabit's tuskers recall the old days when Kenya was roamed by great bulls with

186

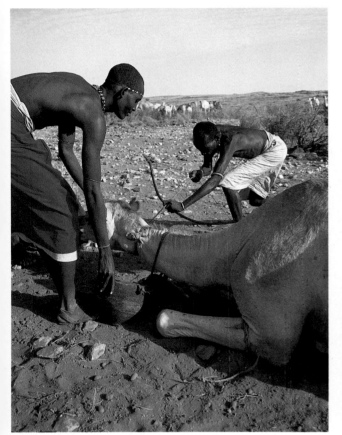

Above: The nomadic Rendille obtain blood from their camels by firing a blunt arrow into the neck. A daub of mud or dung is used to plug the wound.

Above right: Closely related to the Samburu and the Maasai, the Rendille bleed camels instead of cattle for their sustaining diet of milk and blood.

ivory weighing more than 100 kilos a pair. The simulated skin and tusks of Ahmed stand in realistic likeness at the National Museum Headquarters in Nairobi: he was protected during his last years by a special decree of President Kenyatta and guarded around the clock until his death in 1974 from age and disease.

The reserve is also famous for its herds of kudu. These antelopes, once rare in Kenya, have made something of a comeback from the rinderpest epidemic which almost wiped them out at the turn of the century. Weighing between 272 to 317 kilograms, a greater kudu can easily clear two metres at a jump despite its impressive weight. Distinguished by what are among the most magnificent horns in the antelope kingdom, their spiral antlers average around 1.3 metres long, with the record length a fraction under 1.8 metres. Their acute hearing is accentuated by their ability to turn their large rounded ears in almost any direction. These large, slender and elegant antelopes, grey in colour with six to eight prominent vertical white stripes on either flank, raise their tail when alarmed, the white underside serving as a warning. Kudu live out their twelve to fifteen years in small herds or families of four to five, although herds of thirty have been seen. The lesser kudu is a smaller, more graceful version of the greater with more stripes — between eleven to fifteen — down the flank. They prefer much drier country and can go without water for a long time. They are widespread in eastern and northern Kenya.

Higher up misty Marsabit mountain lies another amphitheatre called Lake Paradise. Along the road that takes you there is a dappled glade and a rock pool filled with hyacinth. The water is choked with elephant

187

dung. There is a concrete dam, but no water spills over the slipway, and the pumping station and attendant's house are both empty. Karare is an ages-old water hole for elephants, but then came man to say that this must be his water, too. The dam was built. The pump was installed and a sign put up which said: Admission strictly forbidden. Elephants do not read, and now man has gone away from Karare and once again the water belongs to the beasts of the forest.

Lake Paradise lies in the bowl below an old 500-foot caldera, rimmed with forest trees laced with Spanish moss. On one side, however, the caldera descends almost to lake level. From the air it looks like an eye — the pupil changing hue and tone, the iris sharp and clear and the lid curled, coy and seductive. For four years, in the 1920s, the American naturalists and film makers Martin and Olsa Johnson made their home at Lake Paradise.

Marsabit has other interests. Uncommon desert people meet here on common ground — the Gabbra, Rendille and Borana, attractive but uncompromising pastoralists with fascinating cultures. The Gabbra have a close-knit unity in which whole families of in-laws live together. The Rendille used to be close friends of the Gabbra, but when the Gabbra attacked the Samburu many years ago, this friendship ended and now neither trusts the other.

All, however, have come to terms with their environment, bleak and arid and hot, to a degree of harmony which few peoples could hope to achieve. But it is a hardy existence. They have to dig deep permanent or temporary wells for water for themselves and their herds. One set of wells, owned by the Borana, is known as the Singing Wells. They lie in a dusty valley on the slopes of Marsabit. The wells plunge vertically, fifteen to fifty feet deep. Each morning, the well masons work in mud and water to fashion a quick-drying trough in the harsh forenoon sun. Four men form a human ladder, the lowest one chest-deep in the water below, the second perched on a rocky ledge, the third balanced expertly on two slender poles and the fourth at the top. Three buckets of stitched giraffe hide swing up and down in harmonic rhythm, the human ladder singing a song which sounds like a hymn. The trough fills quickly and the Borana women, with glowing skins and aquiline features, garbed in full-length robes, hair crimped in old-fashioned style, hurry to take home the day's supplies as the beasts drink eagerly. The value the desert people place on these animals is clear. Rather than risk them dying in Marsabit's chill night air, they opt to walk as far as seventy kilometres to the heat of the desert floor before returning in a day or two to water them again.

From Marsabit a road leads across the pitiless glare of the Chalbi Desert through a small outpost called North Horr. The improbable signpost at the edge of the town gives the distance you will travel to reach the eastern shores of Lake Turkana — more than 350 kilometres. For many it may well be the most rewarding journey of their life. For it is within Sibiloi National Park on the shores of Lake Turkana — according to all the evidence uncovered so far — that mankind took his first footsteps, at a place called Koobi Fora.

Even now the forces which shaped Africa's Great Rift Valley are not 188 fully understood. That the fault was caused by an upheaval immense

Above: Proud Boran woman with milk gourd. Centred around Marsabit, Kenya's 80,000-strong Boran belong to a group of Oromo-speaking people who migrated southward from Ethiopia at the end of the last century.

Right: Dassanich girl fills gourd containers with precious water from a dried-up river bed. Also known as the Merille, the Dassanich live on the northern shores of Lake Turkana, around the Omo delta, in both Kenya and Ethiopia.

enough to gouge out a valley that is sometimes 100 kilometres wide and as much as 2,000 feet below the surrounding plains was confirmed by Gregory in 1893. But though Gregory named it the Great Rift, it is the name with which it was endowed by another geologist which best captures the imagination: *graben*, deriving from *grabe*, the grave. In the light of what has been found since, no other image could be more exact.

The tectonic movements which formed the Great Rift Valley established the right formula for preserving fossil bones. These holocausts forced Africa to arch its back, fracturing its vertebrae. Flaming sores erupted on its flesh spewing out the chemical, calcium carbonate, which is capable of transforming bones into fossils. Africa's convulsions were spaced over thousands of years, each spasm causing lakes to form and waters to flow along fresh rills and over new-born plains. Each wrack laid down new sediments from these waters, rising in tiers like different fillings in an exotic cake. Within each tier, tightly compressed in their shrouds of calcium carbonate, lay the skeletons of several species, including the remains of mankind's ancestors.

Finally the frenzy abated and Africa endured a last, long-drawn-out tremor. Its spine collapsed. The Rift was formed. The scarps had tilted and the grave was open. The unique nature of these fossil beds is that erosion has left bones and teeth exposed.

All that was needed was for someone to dig among its bones. Fate might well have given that honour to Lieutenant Ludwig von Hohnel, Count Samuel Teleki's loyal geographer, biographer and friend. While Teleki's sole ambition seems to have been to slaughter East Africa's wildlife, von Hohnel diligently recorded the flora and fauna, the ecology, geology, geography and ethnic constituents which formed this part of East Africa and the Rift Valley.

At the end of March 1888, Teleki's expedition crossed the shores of Lake Turkana at Koobi Fora. Learned though he was, von Hohnel failed to recognize the significance of the landscape. He complained on March 29 of the difficulty of walking across Koobi Fora's sandstone rocks, not thinking to look beneath them. A week later, the tired party approached a Merille settlement at what is probably now Ileret, where two of the

189

main fossil-bearing areas exist. Perhaps the two Austrians stumbled across a similar fossil bed, for von Hohnel records: 'After an hour's walk we issued from the wood which extended in a westerly direction to the side of the lake. Then came a stretch of ground strewn with human skulls and bones.'

It was not to be, however, and it was another eighty years before this area assumed its present significance when, one day in July 1967, Richard Leakey flew along the eastern shores of Lake Turkana. He saw below a tangle of blackened sandstone layers that looked like the slag heaps of a coal pit. Leakey asked the pilot to circle. The single-engined plane made another pass, wheeling out over the water beyond the sandy pit of Koobi Fora, to fly once more over this weird badland at a height of one thousand feet.

A camera could only have recorded this ugly landscape as it is, almost bereft of life. Leakey saw things differently, however — not exactly an hallucination but rather an inspired guess, a vision of the distant past as it might have been. First he saw graceful trees and rolling meadowlands where green grasses and vegetables grew. Mischievous monkeys gambolled in the thick foliage. Strange elephant-like pachyderms with shortened trunks and thicker but smaller tusks browsed quietly. Nearby some hairy people, small but upright, with squat low foreheads, chattered amicably in one group; in another workmen banged and chipped stones to fashion new tools. Now rivers cut through the meadowlands in Leakey's inner eye, waters swift and clear. Eden was spread out before him.

Borrowing a helicopter from the American Omo Valley team, Richard returned to the sandstone hills near Alia Bay to check on what his inspired vision had promised. The helicopter blades had barely stopped whirling when Leakey picked up a stone-age tool similar to those he had found in Olduvai Gorge as a youngster. Within months Richard Leakey assumed the directorship of Kenya's National Museums and began the exploration which confirmed Koobi Fora as the world's richest treasure-trove of fossils of early hominids.

190   Fewer than ten years later, Richard was summoned by his friend

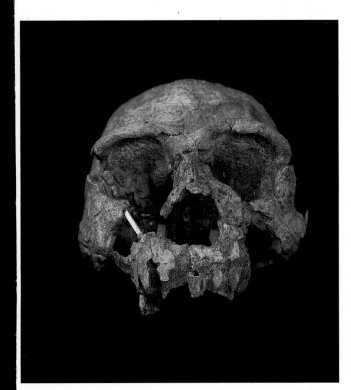

Above: Fossil skull KNM ER 3733 — the remains of Homo erectus *that put back the date of mankind's beginnings by at least half a million years.*
Excavations at Koobi Fora in Sibiloi National Park on the eastern shores of Lake Turkana have given the most significant clues to mankind's origins yet discovered, earning this area of the Rift Valley the title of Cradle of Mankind.

Kamoya Kimeu to a spot on the outlying edges of the Lake Turkana excavations. Richard spent weeks piecing together thirty or more fossil fragments. The result of this painstaking work was another skull similar to that of *Homo habilis*, but dating back almost three million years. Other discoveries of even greater significance have since been made: skulls of *Homo erectus*, the first species of man to walk upright. These discoveries confirm that mankind has been present on earth for at least a million years: 500,000 years longer than was previously believed.

To quicken the pace of discovery, Leakey evolved a new approach to palaeontology involving a multi-disciplinary team of scientists. Doors have been opened to all with the qualities and qualifications to share the work. The result is a unique mix of skills, beliefs and nationalities, making more profound assessments about early human history than could ever have been achieved by one person.

Many prehistoric relics of major importance lie open on the ground. Richard Leakey recounts his discovery of the area's first Australopithecus fossil: 'There on the sand twenty feet ahead, in full view beside a thorny bush, lay a domed grayish-white object. Halfway to it I sat down stunned, incredulous, staring. For years I had dreamed of such a prize, and now I had found it — the nearly complete skull of an early hominid.'

The precise location of each discovery is marked by a concrete post bearing a reference number. The three most important finds are KNM-ER 1470, which is the skull of *Homo habilis*, and KNM-ER 3733 and 3883, the skulls of *Homo erectus*. Visitors to Sibiloi National Park who want to see these sites require special permission from the National Museums of Kenya. The richest era of discovery dates between three million and one million years ago. In the past two decades, more than 160 fossil remains of early hominids, more than 4,000 fossil specimens of mammals, and numerous stone-age artefacts have been recovered. The mammal finds include seventy-five extinct and twelve existing species. Other remains include fish, turtle, tortoise and crocodile species.

It is not just the fossils which have given Koobi Fora significance. The sedimentary layers in which the fossils were buried have yielded important evidence of the environment three million years ago and of the animals and plants with which early man and pre-man shared the world.

Leakey believes there is enough evidence to establish that Lake Turkana's shores were once a well-watered verdant land of forest and grass blessed with an abundance of good things. The plains teemed with wild animals including prehistoric elephants, three-toed ancestors of the horse, sabre-toothed cats, extra-large antelopes, giant baboons, rhino-sized pigs, odd-looking ostriches and many other strange ancestors of modern species.

From the deck of a fishing boat anchored in Alia Bay, the unblinking eye of a sleeping crocodile reflects red in the beam of a torch. It has survived 130 million years and witnessed, not so long ago by its time span, those first footsteps of ours.

Perhaps indeed this was Eden where human life began. And, perhaps, indeed, all life, all things bright and beautiful, wild and wonderful, are out of Kenya.